West Coast Steelheader

Introduction by Barry M. Thornton
Matt Guiguet
Steve Kaye
Art Lingren
David Murphy

Compiled by Mark Pendlington

ISBN 0-88839-459-4
Copyright © 2000 Ocean West Group Ltd.

Cataloging in Publication Data
Main entry under title:
West Coast steelheader

Includes index.
  ISBN 0-88839-459-4

  1. Steelhead fishing—British Columbia.
I. Pendlington, Mark. II. Guiguet, Matt.
SH687.7.W47 2000   799.1'757'08711   C99-910796-8

We acknowledge the financial support of the Government of Canada through the Book Publishing Industry Development Program for our publishing activities.

Editor: Nancy Miller
Production: Ingrid Luters
Principal photographer: All photography by Harry Penner unless otherwise noted.
Illustrator: Ian Forbes
Knot patterns: Harry Nilsson

The authors' royalties for West Coast Steelheader *will be donated to steelhead enhancement projects in British Columbia.*

Published simultaneously in Canada and the United States by

HANCOCK HOUSE PUBLISHERS LTD.
19313 Zero Avenue, Surrey, B.C. V4P 1M7

HANCOCK HOUSE PUBLISHERS
1431 Harrison Avenue, Blaine, WA 98230-5005

(604) 538-1114   Fax (604) 538-2262
(800) 938-1114   Fax (800) 983-2262
Web Site: www.hancockhouse.com   *email:* sales@hancockhouse.com

Contents

Ian forbes

Preface

The first fifteen minutes were spent getting comfortable with the pristine surroundings. Steelhead green water passed through some of the nicest steelhead runs I had ever seen—walking-pace flow with large boulders tapering out to base-ball-sized rocks at the tailout—totalling about a seventy-five-foot piece of fishable water.

My fishing partner was the first to touch a steelhead. It was a chrome-bright doe that weighed about five pounds. Within about half a minute the tail-slashing, water-boiling dance was over.

I positioned myself a little further up the river on the next run. This run was a narrow section separated by boulders that divided the river into fishable water and a truly spectacular 300-foot run that hugged a tree-strewn bank. The river ranged from two- to five-foot depths with a number of obvious steel-head-holding waters. I climbed over fallen old-growth cedars and thick brush to reach the head of the run.

I adjusted my float length to about six feet, hooked a spawn sac onto my #2 hook and threw my offering in the first fishable part of the run. As I held back slightly on the float, the spawn sac bounced within inches of the bottom. As the bait floated further away, I began to contemplate the difficulties of trying to land a steelhead here. I was perched on an old cedar stump, surrounded by branches about ten feet above the water. Wham! That's when I felt the strike.

Totally unprepared, I felt the line tighten, and the rod pounded into a perfect arc. I curved the rod to the side and held the fish out of the debris and branches that were all along the bank. The fish held fast in the current. It appeared to be a male steelhead of about twelve pounds. As the rose color on the side of the steelhead disappeared into the whitewater, the line ripped against my thumb as he went through a series of quick runs and acrobatic, rolling jumps. Snap!

I looked around helplessly, somewhere between steel-head heaven and total exasperation.

I vividly remember every steelhead I have seen; no two are exactly alike, each having slightly different colorations or markings. I am still in awe of the majestic summer and winter steelhead and the West Coast rivers that they call home. After five seasons of filming the *Sportfishing British Columbia* television series I have had the extreme privilege of steelheading with some of the most successful summer and winter steelhead anglers on the West Coast.

Professional guide David Murphy has led his clients to more steelhead than any guide in British Columbia—at last count it was over four thousand. In his chapter "Natural Baits for Winter and Summer Steelhead" Dave shares his practical no nonsense steelheading expertise that will help you to become a better steelheader. He explains his professional guiding techniques covering all aspects of natural baits, floats and weight systems, curing roe and river fishing strategies to get you steelheading with the pros.

In the chapter "Artificials for Winter and Summer Steelhead" professional South Coast guide Steve Kaye knows of what he speaks. I have had some incredible steelheading days on some of the most heavily fished steelhead rivers on the West Coast with him. Steve narrows down the infinite number of possibilities that you will need to adapt to for success on the river. He covers all aspects of artificial baits: what to use, where steelhead hold in a river, float fishing, bottom bouncing, weight systems, lines, short float systems and covering water.

In "Plug Fishing for Steelhead" professional guide Matt Guiguet shares his lifelong obsession with steelheading on West Coast rivers. Matt discusses everything you need to know to effectively plug for steelhead: where to fish in a river, back trolling techniques, how fish approach the plug, drift boats, tuning, distancing, strike zones, when to fish plugs, plug sizes and colors and the rods that are best for plugging.

One of the most difficult challenges in angling on the West Coast would have to be taking a winter or summer run steelhead on a fly. In his chapter "Fly Fishing for Winter and Summer Steelhead" author Art Lingren has written, in my opinion, five thousand of the most concise and unbiased words written on the subject of steelhead to the fly on the

West Coast. Every fly angler will develop their own favorite flies and techniques in time, but Art provides a foundation for understanding the rich history of steelhead flyfishers on the west Coast, the rivers, flies, techniques and equipment. I felt Art Lingren's chapter was worthy of being reprinted from the *West Coast Fly Fisher* book. It forms the basis for a larger understanding of the steelhead obsession that you will no doubt develop all by yourself.

I thank author Barry Thornton for writing the introduction to summer and winter steelhead which includes background discussion of the steelhead ranging from the steelhead's migrating paths to its biological importance. I would also like to thank Ian Forbes for the beautiful pencil illustrations of summer and winter steelhead an Harry Nilsson for the attention to detail provided in the knot illustrations.

It is my hope that the following pages of this book will make you a better steelheader and give you the most important element in the evolution of becoming a West Coast steelheader, realizing that summer and winter steelhead are much more than just another fish—they are a barometer of a river system's health. With some rivers of the Pacific Northwest at dangerously low steelhead population levels, learning the right time and correct way to use natural bait, flies or artificials will drastically improve your success in catching and releasing these magnificent fish unharmed to complete their incredible life cycle.

This book is filled with concise information and beautiful full color pictures that truly are a celebration of the steelhead and the rivers of the west coast with exacting descriptions from the authors you will want to read it again and again. This book removes the mystery and informs and motivates you to know steelhead better.

MARK PENDLINGTON

An Introduction to Winter and Summer Steelhead

The Pacific Coast is home to one of North America's most exciting and challenging freshwater sports fish—the steelhead trout. The steelhead is a seagoing or anadromous species of rainbow (Kamloops) trout. Until the late 1980s it had the scientific name, *Salmo gairdneri richardson*. However, the American Fisheries Society (AFS) recognized that the Kamchatka or Asian steelhead race had a historic previous subspecies label, mykiss; hence, all steelhead and rainbow trout now have the name mykiss. At about that same time, the AFS determined that there was no biological reason for separating rainbow trout from Pacific salmon at the generic level. Therefore they labeled all trout and salmon of Pacific lineage in the same genus, *Oncorhynchus*. Today, steelhead throughout the world are known as *Oncorhynchus mykiss*.

Steelhead have two distinct races, winter steelhead and summer steelhead—so named because of the season these fish enter their home streams. Winter steelhead begin ascending their natal streams as early as November. Runs of these fish continue to enter their rivers from November through April and some rivers actually have winter steelhead going into their systems as late as June. Summer steelhead begin to enter their home rivers in June and continue through October.

Summer and winter steelhead have distinct behavioral differences. Summer steelhead have been known to feed when they enter their natal river and can be attracted to strike by color and lure activity. Winter steelhead on the other hand rarely feed when they enter their home stream although they have been known to ingest objects (worms, feathers, leaf material and salmon eggs) if the items drift past their snout.

Spawning for both races occurs throughout the late winter months and early spring in fist-sized gravel. Temperature is the key factor that determines when the eggs hatch and when the yolk-bellied alevin break free to grow among the river-bottom gravel. Once the young steelhead use up their yolk food reserves they squirm up through the gravel and become free-swimming fry. They live in their home stream for two, three or even four years before they enter the smolt stage and migrate downstream to the ocean. Prior to reaching the ocean they silver-up (while in fresh-water phase the smolts have faint markings similar to a small rainbow trout) adapting to the osmotic change that will occur when their body moves from a fresh-water environment to saltwater.

In the ocean, our Pacific steelhead migrate north along the continental shelf; then in a great eastern/southern crescent around the Gulf of Alaska; then, south along the shelf of the Aleutian Island chain to a vast marshaling ground near 50°N latitude and 170°W longitude. Here in this immense area of the Pacific Ocean they mingle with steelhead from other North American streams and their Asian cousins from streams on the Kamchatka Peninsula. When the urge to migrate back to their home streams occurs, they reverse their journey or make a direct line back to North American shores, then travel south until they reach the estuary of their home stream.

Steelhead are generally loners, fish that travel by themselves except for opportunistic feeding times when they will find themselves in the company of other steelhead and Pacific salmon. When they reach their natal river mouth they will stay in the estuary until water conditions like those present during a rain storm or freshet occur, which will draw them up the river. Once in the river they travel slowly, usually in the evening or early morning, or during overcast days.

Some steelhead are wanderers, in fact, nearly 20 percent wander to spawn in streams other then their home river. This wandering is the way that steelhead have historically populated streams and the manner in which genetic viability has occurred.

Spawning is the ultimate purpose of all steelhead. It is their reason for being. Unlike Pacific salmon, which die after spawning, steelhead are able to reverse the chemical and physical changes that occur in their body prior to the spawning act. Some will survive to spawn a second and even a rare third time.

Spawning occurs when the doe or hen steelhead locates a suitable gravel area at the tailout of a pool. She turns her body sideways and then in a sigmoid (S-shape) action she snaps her tail upward sucking the gravel out from its bed where the current will take it downstream. She repeats this a number of times in one location and then spawns between 500 and 2,000 eggs in this first depression. The male, or buck, spawns his sperm at the same time, knowing from the excitement of the doe that she is spawning. Often two or more male steelhead will spawn at that precise moment beside the doe. After the first spawn the doe moves upstream and once again, using the sygmoid body shape, she prepares another depression for a second spawn. The gravel from the second depression drifts downstream to cover the first spawning. This process is repeated until the doe has spawned her approximate 6,000 eggs.

After spawning, steelhead are refereed to as kelts. In this emaciated state they drift downstream often feeding voraciously on any foods available. For them it quickly becomes a race to reach the ocean food and many do not survive this trying time. But, for those that do, the ocean offers a smorgasbord of feed and the salt water quickly mends the infections and sores that were sustained while in fresh water.

The life history of the steelhead is a fascinating story. Their's is a complex journey in a watery medium that is only now being unraveled as scientists discover more and more about this valuable marine species. We now recognize that the steelhead is a barometer of the health of watersheds and of the ocean. Their journey is a lifelong odyssey full of fascination and adventure. Their existence provides a valuable recreational resource for the steelheader. For the angler, steelheading is an adventure that is also full of fascination and excitement for a powerful river trout with an average weight of eight pounds. But, many steelhead have weights in the teens, the twenties and even the thirties. These latter fish are the trophies that bring anglers from all over the world to fish British Columbia's 500-plus known steelhead streams.

The Pacific Northwest provides a wealth of angling opportunities for the steelheader. The region has been blessed with many summer and winter races of both wild and hatchery fish. The sheer power and excitement that these fish have to offer make it the supreme trophy trout. Enjoy it!

BARRY M. THORNTON

Artificials for Winter and Summer Steelhead

by Steve Kaye

I had been fishing hard all day and had not found any steelhead. It was about 2:30 on a late February afternoon and it had been cold for a couple of weeks, there was even some snow along the riverbank. The river was gin clear and fairly low. I decided to fish a run in the upper river that had produced well for me previously, but with low, clear conditions it could also prove to be void of any willing fish. I approached the river slowly from the tailout of the run. The sun was situated such that with my Polaroid glasses I could see every rock on the bottom. I slowly walked and scanned the run coming to the top section where the water deepened to approximately six feet with a little surface chop. It was more difficult to see the bottom but as I stood quietly observing the movement of the water through a small surface window that appeared from time to time, I was able to detect the subtle movement of a tail fin!

I positioned myself approximately fifteen feet upstream from the fish and retied my leader with fresh six-pound line and a #2 hook. I figured a small Jensen egg and a wisp of yarn would be pretty tempting. I readjusted my float to approximately five and a half feet and made my cast about twenty feet in front of the fish to avoid spooking him and to allow my gear to sink and position itself properly. Once the float hit the water, I picked up the slack line with my single-action reel and drew a tight line to the float. Feathering line off the spool, I allowed the float to drift down the seam that held the steelhead. As the float drifted past the position of the holding fish, it dipped under the water. I came back hard on my rod to set the hook and after a half-second pause I felt the heavy head shakes and saw the flashing of a large steelhead. (For me this is the best part—that first second or two of the hookup time almost stand still.) After the usual combination of runs and one good jump, the fish lay in the shallows at my feet—approximately fifteen pounds of wild steelhead. I quickly revived the steelhead and it took off like a shot. A successful day of steelhead fishing.

Many different details go into a successful steelhead outing. But that is the point of the matter, float fishing is about attention to details. On any given day there are an infinite number of possibilities that need to be perceived and adapted to for success. It is my sincere hope that the words that follow will help you solve on a more consistent basis the wonderful, challenging puzzle that is steelhead.

About Baits

As with any type of fishing, during float fishing there is more emphasis placed on what kind of bait to use than any other aspect of the fishing. However, what you put on your hook is only one part of the riddle. The most important characteristic of any bait is that the angler has confidence in it. Steelhead can be caught on a myriad of offerings, so with this in mind let us not limit ourselves—let us not get carried away either! Personally, over the course of the day I will switch periodically between three or four different baits depending on the situation and conditions at hand. The one common denominator between them is that I have confidence in each bait presented.

Organic Baits

While there is no shortage of artificial baits available for float fishing, it is often hard to beat good natural bait. Salmon and steelhead are very susceptible to roe, spawn sacks, ghost shrimp, prawns and even dew worms. One of the advantages of natural baits over artificial baits is the tendency for fish to hold on to them longer, giving the angler a better chance to set the hook. Each bait has its own different characteristics and application.

Roe is probably the most widely used natural bait for steelhead and salmon. There are many commercially available ways to cure your bait from natural to almost fluorescent red colors. (Curing is described fully in the chapter on natural baits.) Personally, I find bright colors work better for salmon, but for steelhead I prefer a more natural-looking bait. Regular borax also makes a great natural bait cure.

Spawn sacks are a great bait because they are easy and trouble free to use. They are cured single eggs tied in a fine mesh sack and all you do is just stick them on your hook. They last much longer in the water than straight roe and are much less messy.

Dew worms can be a good alternative bait for steelhead and salmon. While not widely used, they can fool a fish that has seen and rejected several other baits.

Prawns are used mostly for steelhead. They make a good, fairly durable bait. Whole or just the tails work well. Try curing them in some of the brightly colored bait cures available on the market. This can really add to their appeal.

Ghost shrimp are a hot bait for steelhead and sometimes salmon. While these little creatures are fragile and go bad quickly, they can definitely be worth the trouble to obtain and fish them.

Organic baits may not be legal on all water systems. It is up to the angler to know what is permitted. Many people have expressed concern for fish caught on organic baits because they feel the fish are hooked deeply. In my experience I have found that this rarely happens. If you do hook a fish deeply and do want to release it, cut the line as close to the hook as possible. Do not try to remove a deeply taken hook. Most fish, if handled properly, will be just fine.

Yarn

Probably the most basic and effective steelhead bait around is yarn. This material is available in more colors that anyone could ever use, and this selection of color also lends itself to incredible versatility. It is easy to rig yarn properly, yet it is often rigged poorly thereby reducing its effectiveness. For rigging and fishing a proper yarn fly, a shank knot is preferred to a bait loop because the shank knot will slide up the shank of the hook and pinch the yarn at the top of the hook right below the eye. When I rig my yarn, I cut three one-inch strands of yarn; I then cinch them tight in the loop and trim them round to represent an egg. One small tip—carry a pair of the fly-tying scissors to aid in trimming, the difference in the finished bait is significant and worth the effort. I also like to incorporate contrast; I almost never make my yarn flies just one color. I always use two or three different shades of yarn and believe this detail of contrast is important. Think about it—everything a fish has ever eaten in its whole life whether it was a minnow, a shrimp, a bug or even an egg is made up of more than one color. I think it makes sense to incorporate this into yarn flies.

Another nice feature of yarn is its size versatility. One can adapt on location to the size required by the conditions at hand. Yarn also accepts the addition of scent products very well, which can at times aid in fishing success. Yarn is also a great way to enhance other baits. Gooey bob's, Jensen eggs, corkies and spin-n-glows as well as organic baits are very enticing and effective when fished with yarn. But the one question I get asked above all is what color works the best. You can ask a dozen different anglers that question and you'll likely get a dozen different answers. The moral of the story is go prepared. Yarn is a cheap and versatile bait. I carry about a dozen different colors in my vest at all times, but most importantly I fish the colors that I have confidence in.

Gooey Bobs

If I had to pick one bait most often associated with steelhead fishing, it would be the gooey bob. This is basically a hunk of plastic that is shaped like an egg cluster. These baits are available in every size, shape and color imaginable. The gooey bob is an excellent bait when visibility is important as their bright colors and obvious profile make them a standout. A key to remember, because of their shape and usually firm composition, gooey bobs should be used with a relatively large hook or you won't get a good piece of the fish when it takes your bait.

Jensen Eggs

Jensen eggs or small rubber eggs are a great bait for delicate presentations in low or very clear water conditions. Some of these baits are scented and others are not. Color selection is almost unlimited. These baits look great when complemented with light-colored yarn. Another little trick is to tie four or six of them in a spawn sack, and remember to vary the colors for contrast. This makes a good roelike presentation in places where organic baits are banned.

Spin-n-Glows

I don't know an avid steelheader who does not at some time or place use spin-n-glows. I must say, they probably even rival the gooey bob for most recognizable steelhead bait. Again size and color selection is almost unlimited. Alone or with bait, these whirling creations really catch fish. Small sizes work well in low, clear water conditions; larger sizes work well in high, off-colored water. Remember to fish them below a swivel and to place a small salmon bead between them and the hook. This will allow the spin-n-glow to spin freely and eliminate line twist.

Blades

Blades are simple spinners constructed with a spinner blade, two swivels, a split ring and a hook. For those new to float fishing it may seem odd to fish this type of lure beneath a float. This technique offers several advantages over fishing the same lure without a float. First, you can suspend your lure above the bottom and reduce lost gear; second, you can vary your presentation. A blade can be dead drifted by just letting the current take and naturally flutter the spinner, and it can be held back during the drift causing the blade to vibrate and flash aggressively. It can also be swung through the run to cover water quickly.

The spinner blades that make up these simple lures come in a variety of shapes, finishes and colors and can be very effective in a variety of water conditions. This is a bait that usually tends to elicit a strike very quickly. I feel a good strategy is to consider blades as a "cleanup" bait. Fish your selected run methodically and carefully with a couple of other baits, if no fish are hooked change to a blade and fish it through quickly covering all the good spots a couple of times. If an active fish is around, they don't need much coaxing. If they fancy a blade be ready, the strike is obvious and aggressive.

Rubber Worms

I saved the best for last. I love fishing worms. No question about it, if you are not fishing rubber worms, you are passing up fish. If a steelhead wants a worm, he will almost always take it in the first few casts. I have had many days of fishing where I had spent an hour fishing several other baits through a run with no success until I tried a worm. On occasion, before leaving a spot to fish elsewhere I have put on a worm and within ten casts have hooked up to three fish in the same spot that previously produced nothing.

The worms come in many colors and sizes. A few different variations prerigged for a quick change allow you to fish worms more conveniently and efficiently. Many anglers feel that worms work better in water that has some color to it and I feel to a large extent this is true. Having said that, I have caught many steelhead in clear water on a brightly colored six-inch worm. So don't be afraid to try them even in clear conditions. I feel that worms are the type of lure that needs to be fished as a cleanup bait. I have had other anglers tell me that they haven't had much success with worms. But remember, you don't need to spend too much time when fishing a worm in a run. The key to success is to fish them fast and fish them last.

Floats

Now that we have covered the various baits available for steelhead, we need to discuss the terminal gear that makes up the rest of the package and allows us to present our baits to the fish. First and most obvious is the float. I feel that this piece of tackle's importance is not fully realized by most anglers. The float is a window of information as to what is happening down below at the business end.

15

Much like a bait, your float can and should be adapted by size and style to match a particular situation. Not all floats are created equal, and quite honestly we could probably write another book on float design and application. Personally, I like my floats to be as sensitive as possible. I prefer a slim, long float to a short, fat model because I feel they have greater sensitivity. For clear or low water, I prefer my floats to be as inconspicuous as possible. I feel a clear float or a light or pale finish is truly an advantage.

Selecting the right size is very important for proper float performance. If more than a quarter of your float is visible during a drift, then you either have too large a float or not enough weight. In many fishing circumstances I will adjust my float and weight combination so I will only have one-half to one-quarter inch above the surface of the water. This provides me with maximum sensitivity and quick strike detection.

Floats come in an abundance of styles and colors, as is shown in the picture section on page 37. It is worth investing some time to experiment with this part of your tackle as it will refine and improve your success.

Mainline

Before going any further, we need to discuss the mainline or the line that we have on the reel. BUY QUALITY LINE! I cannot stress this enough. It is just not worth the hassle, not to mention lost fish, to save a couple of bucks. There are many good quality fishing lines on the market today, and each has its own characteristics. You will just have to try a few and find the one that is right for your angling style. Line test should be between twelve and twenty pounds. This will depend on location, conditions, equipment and personal preference. I find for most applications fifteen-pound test mainline is just about right.

Weight Systems

Once an angler has determined what type of float and mainline they are going to fish, they must then decide how they are going to weight their line—yes, it does make a difference.

There are two basic types of weighting systems in use today. Both have a time and a place.

The first, and probably the most popular, weight system is "deep-line" rigging. This is accomplished by weighting our mainline just above the swivel. A piece of hollow core pencil lead is the most popular method and can be attached several ways. Surgical tubing, dropper lines and snubber systems are all good methods, but my favorite way of using pencil lead is probably the simplest method of all. All you do is cut the lead to size using a pair of wire strippers, this prevents the hole that runs down the center of the lead from being crushed when cut. Then just thread your line directly through the lead and tie on your bottom swivel. The lead rests on the swivel and does not damage your line or your knot. Pencil lead can be purchased very inexpensively in one-pound rolls and cut to size as needed.

Another twist on deep-line weighting systems is to use a weight called a slinky. These weights are simply a length of parachute cord filled with steel shot or lead balls. While these weights do not get snagged-up quite as often as regular pencil lead, they do give up some "bottom feel" that pencil lead provides.

There is another style of weight, which I call the "short-float" system. This involves the use of simple split shot attached to your line at varying distances from the swivel on up. The short-float system allows for an extremely natural drift, but don't get too close to the bottom with split shot or you'll likely be retying as these weights tend to hang up often. Split shot is available in magnum size to extra-extra tiny, so you can adjust to any situation that requires this type of delicate presentation.

Rods and Reels

I prefer to fish a center pin reel with a click and drag system, which allows me to feather the mainline off the spool to a custom thirteen-foot, center-pin noodlerod. This provides me with the ultimate in control and sensitivity, and a rod with enough power to handle a large steelhead. The popular choice for most steelheading applications would be a good graphite rod between ten and a half and twelve feet in length, with a high-quality level wind reel that has a dependable star-drag system.

Leaders, Swivels and Hooks

Last, but not least, is the business end of our rigging—the swivel, leader and hook.

Barrel swivels or three-way swivels in sizes 8 to 14 fit the bill nicely. I prefer size 14 black, barrel swivels for most of my applications rather than gold or silver because I don't want to distract the fish from the really important part of the rig.

Before we get to the hook, there is still one more essential piece to our rigging. Leaders are made up of regular pieces of monofilament, but test strength, diameter and length selection of the leader can be critical. Rule of thumb: clear water is light and long (6–10 lb. and 30–40 in. length); dirty water heavy and short (12–20 lb. and 10–25 in. length). And anywhere in between as conditions demand. A point of interest, I have in the last couple of seasons been experimenting with a leader material called fluorocarbon. It is manufactured by several different companies and, quite honestly, is expensive. However, when this leader material is immersed in water, it becomes almost invisible because it hardly refracts any light. I have found on bright days in clear water this can at times make the difference on picky fish. Leaders should always be inspected regularly and retied if they show even the slightest abrasions.

Two things I never go cheap on are fishing line and hooks. BUY ONLY QUALITY HOOKS! They are just too important. Octopus or steelhead style hooks are preferred. Hook size should be matched to the bait and conditions—big bait, big hook; small bait, small hook. Typical hook sizes for float fishing will range from a small size #6 to as large as a #4/0. Something that many anglers overlook is the color or finish of their hook. Most come in a variety of colors, this is a small detail but a successful day's fishing sometimes is about small details. For instance, I never use a silver hook if I am float fishing for salmon, particularly coho. But I do find steelhead like that little sparkle that comes off a silver hook. Experiment for yourself!

The Details of Float Fishing

Details and the attention to them are what make successful anglers. It doesn't matter how much you know about what bait, style of float or weight to use, if you don't know how or when to fish it properly you won't be very successful. The attention to details of how you fish is just as important and often more important than what you fish. Do not forget another important factor—the fish. We first have to find him or her. Being consistently successful requires a keen knowledge of the water system you are fishing. The more you know about your favorite river's sweet spots, the more fish you will catch.

Following is one of the most important secrets of any good steelheader—cover water! Sounds simple I know, but this is very important. The more spots you fish in a day, the better off you will be for two reasons. First, you will increase your odds of showing your bait to more fish. Second, as you move from spot to spot, you will increase your working knowledge of the river.

Be alert! You can learn a lot by simply watching. If you see an angler catch a fish, take note of where. Fish tend to hold in the same spots as long as water conditions remain relatively consistent. You may see a fish porpoise or you just may see a fish holding in the water. Something I always have with me and most likely on me when I'm fishing is a good pair of Polaroid glasses. They are three good reasons for wearing Polaroids. First, they help you spot fish. I've caught many fish because I was able to see them in the water. Second, they help you read the water better. You can interpret currents and make out bottom structure and contour much better, which can help you find fish. And third, they reduce or eliminate surface glare, which makes it easier to track your float and reduces eye fatigue and possible headache.

Many anglers have a difficult time recognizing good holding water. Fish definitely prefer certain places in rivers over others. Steelhead require two basic elements from any holding spot—comfort and security. These two requirements will also vary a little with each individual fish.

Comfort comes in the form of water speed. Typically walking speed water is preferred. But if water temperatures are low (as in winter), the fish may prefer slower water. And conversely, if the water temperature is up (as in spring or summer), you may find them in slightly faster water.

Security comes from cover. This has many variables. Cover can be an undercut bank, a deep hole, behind a boulder or under surface chop. Log jams and current seams also do nicely. Combine security and comfort and you will usually find steelhead.

Steelhead holding water takes on many shapes and sizes, regardless, covering the water thoroughly is important. Making the exact same drift in the same spot over and over again is unnecessary and a waste of time. What you want to accomplish is complete coverage of all good holding water. Covering water is relatively simple but very important. Essentially, what you are trying to implement is a systematic approach to showing every fish in a given spot your bait several times. Starting at the top of your fishing spot and make a short cast to the closest area of good holding water, make a moderate drift and then on your second attempt increase your cast by about one foot and keep repeating this until the section in front of you has been covered. Remember, it is not necessary or effective to make long drifts—keep it short, approximately twenty to fifty feet at a time. After you are satisfied that the water in front of you has been covered well, take one or two steps downstream and start the procedure again. As you repeat this process, every possible spot that a fish may be holding in will be covered. You may want to repeat this whole process with a couple of different baits giving the fish in front and below you a couple of different choices. I hope you caught that tip, water coverage and changing up your bait is another secret of successful steelheaders. If you grow roots in one spot and make the same drift with the same bait all day, your window of opportunity is only open just a crack.

Of all the pieces of the float fishing puzzle, the following is the most important. It has nothing to do with what bait or float you are using or your favorite fishing hole. This is about how your bait looks to the fish in the water.

The single-most important part of your approach to float fishing for steelhead and salmon is the presentation of your bait. While the word presentation is used frequently by the fly-fishing fraternity, float fishers seldom even say it. In my opinion, this is the most important aspect of float fishing, and there are several different and important aspects involved. Keep in mind the fish does not care if your rod costs $50 or $500, he doesn't care what you're wearing, all he needs to care about is your bait. All of your equipment and tackle should be focused on the one point, how the fish sees your offerings. This will ultimately decide if he bites it or not. Now don't get me wrong, this isn't brain surgery and most steelhead (or salmon for that matter) have a brain the size of a quarter. What we have to do as anglers is consider our bait from the fish's perspective. What a fish wants to see is a drift that is as natural as possible. Most fish in rivers prefer to see their food coming to them in the current in a natural, free-floating manner. It is this drift we are trying to emulate. Slow water is more demanding than fast water. In slow water a fish has a lot of time to observe your bait, so your presentation has to be on the money. In faster drifts it is often an advantage to slow down your bait slightly in relation to the current speed. This gives the fish more time to make a decision to take the bait.

There are many factors that make a good presentation. One of the first things to remember is that your float is your window to the fish's world and you need to learn how to interpret what your float is telling you. One of the most common and most obvious mistakes that I see anglers make is that they cast too far upstream. In doing this, you have no control over your drift. Your bait inevitably ends up being dragged behind your weight and float. This does not look natural at all. Ideally, what an angler should do is cast slightly upstream. Once your gear hits the water you want to pick up the slack line, because if your line is allowed to stay on the surface it will create a bow in the line and cause your gear to be unnaturally dragged along. As soon as you have a tight line to your float, you want to gently allow line off your reel, now this is the most important part of your drift. If you let the line feed off too quickly, your bait gets towed downstream by the float. If you hold the line back too much, you will pull your bait away from the bottom creating drag. This looks unnatural and is not very effective. There is a fine line between a natural, free-floating bait and a poor, unnatural-looking presentation. Another mistake anglers make is drifts that are far too long. Keep your drifts short, approximately twenty to fifty feet at a time. Long drifts are hard to control and result in a poor presentation. Only one thing can help you determine if you're fishing effectively and that is practice. Nothing beats time spent on the river.

For the most part, when fishing for winter steelhead and most salmon species, it is thought that bait must be presented right at the bottom of the river or eye level to the fish. The best method of float fishing in this manner is the deep-line method. As discussed earlier, this involves the use of pencil lead attached just above your swivel. This is a great way to get your bait down to where the fish are holding. You will want to adjust your float so your weight makes bottom contact every three to six feet of drift. Remember to keep the line that extends to the float off of the water. Your float should be just slightly leaning in your direction as you make your drift and you should feel your weight just ticking the bottom every few feet. You should see the float bob slightly every time your weight touches the bottom. As you fish your way through a run, keep your drifts short, and as you move down the run it may be necessary to adjust your float depth from time to time as the river bottom and depth are constantly changing. Ideally, we want to present the bait at or slightly slower than current speed and at the fish's eye level in order to give it time to see the bait and not have to move far to pick it up. Remember, attention to detail and keeping in mind the fish's point of view is what we are trying to accomplish with this style of float fishing.

The deep-line method works extremely well for steelhead and salmon under a variety of conditions. When water quality is poor, this method keeps your bait in the fish's site zone and when water temperatures are low, such as occurs in

November, December, January, February and sometimes March, fish will seldom move off the bottom to intercept a bait. Pocket water and current seams are also great places to use this format, as you need to get your bait into position quickly and slow it down to give the fish time to decide to take it.

During the summer, early fall and late spring, water temperatures rise and the fish become very active and even aggressive. At these times of year steelhead will rise off the bottom and move to or even chase a bait. As long as water clarity is good, say a minimum of six to eight feet of visibility, I prefer to use the short-float method of fishing. As discussed earlier, the short float technique involves the use of split shot instead of pencil lead. The main advantage for using split shot is that it provides a very natural drift. Slow to medium water speeds work best for this technique.

It is not important that we be right on the bottom. In fact, we are actually trying to avoid contact with the river bottom. Steelhead during these seasons really seem to be looking up and are ready and waiting to come up and get bait. I know this sounds a little odd for many steelhead anglers as many believe steelhead are only on the bottom and the bait then must also be on the bottom. This is true for winter-run fish but summer-run, fall-run and even spring-run steelhead will rise up or even chase bait that they want. Now, I'm not suggesting that we adjust our baits to be just below the surface. What we want to do is adjust our float and weight combination so that our bait is suspended one to three feet above the riverbed. You don't need to hold back much on the float, just lift the line off the water and guide your bait though the run. A nice dead drift is what we are trying to achieve. When we are fishing in this manner there are a few distinct advantages. First, because we are not right on the river bottom, we do not lose nearly as much gear; therefore, we don't have as much wasted time retying or the expense. But the best part of short floating is that when the float drops it's almost always a fish! Because the fish has to rise and get the bait, once he grabs it he will immediately start to return to the river bottom. This instantly drops the float and usually pulls the hook into the corner of the fish's mouth. This actually increases your landing percentages because you tend to hook the fish better.

When choosing your baits for short floating, select baits that have some weight to them. This allows them to drop below the split shot and looks more natural during a dead drift. Rubber worms, blades, gooey bobs and organic baits, such as roe, spawn sacks or sand shrimp, are perfect for the short-float technique.

Wrapping it Up

I remember the first season or two that I started float fishing rivers for steelhead and salmon was tough sledding, to put it mildly. I live in the Fraser Valley, so one of the rivers I fished often was the Chilliwack/Vedder River. I watched other anglers catch coho, springs and steelhead all around me, but none seemed to like what I had to offer. Even though I was fishing the exact same gear as they were (or so I thought), I was rarely successful. Fortunately, I tend to be persistent in nature and I embraced the challenge to learn how to float fish properly.

There are two sayings that over the years I have found to be true. The first is 10 percent of the anglers catch 90 percent of the fish; second, if you can consistently catch steelhead in the Chilliwack River you can catch them anywhere. I feel both of these statements go together and the truth within them can be universally applied to any stream or river anywhere. Many anglers who float fish only occasionally and don't observe or learn more about this technique are rarely successful on a consistent basis. The more you rely on luck, the less fish you will catch. Float fishing is the type of technique that if done well is deadly, but if done poorly is almost useless and very frustrating—it's just not very forgiving.

In many ways float fishing and fly fishing have a lot in common. Obviously there are substantial differences in tackle and technique, but the attention to presentation and the details that make it work are what make them similar. Most fly fishermen have been experimenting with and fishing subtle advancements with tackle and flies for years, in fact volumes have been written about the subject. I feel this attitude can and should be adopted and adapted by float fisherman. If there is any doubt as to the level one can take float fishing all you have to do is check out some of the float fishing techniques the British use to catch carp, it may just surprise you.

Becoming a successful float fisherman is about attitude. You have to have an open mind. You can learn so much from others. Everyone has his or her own style for sure, but remember everything has a time and place and there is an exception to every rule. Another variable to consider is that every river system is different with its own distinct personality. Certain baits are more consistent producers in certain river systems than others and no two seasons are the same. Rivers are constantly changing; you must always be exploring. Your favorite fishing hole will not last forever. Very few rivers remain the same year after year. I have been very fortunate to have fished all over British Columbia. I have caught fish on Vancouver Island, the Fraser River and many of its tributaries, the Skeena River system and even in a couple rivers in the Nass system. While each river has its own definite personality, the basic principles and the need for attention to detail are consistent.

Most of what has been previously discussed pertains to catching steelhead, but don't limit yourself. These fishing techniques and strategies are deadly on other species as well. I have caught many cutthroat, dolly varden and all five species of salmon while float fishing. In fact, salmon season is a great time of year to start float fishing as the numbers are more in your favor. There can be thousands of fish available to catch and nothing helps you learn to catch fish faster than catching fish.

Fishing in all its forms is a wonderful thing. Many people are content to relax and catch the odd fish, others want to take it to another level beyond that of an occasional hobby. For many dedicated anglers, fishing is an integral part of their life, for some fishing is their life. Regardless of what priority one puts on fishing, ultimately fishing is supposed to be fun. Whatever level you take it to, don't lose sight of this. Fishing is about the experiences, the challenges and the memories it creates.

Natural Baits for Winter and Summer Steelhead

by David Murphy

With competition on the rivers growing every year due to new generations of steelhead fishermen, the quests for steelhead and new ways to catch them have intensified. In recent years anglers have had a hard time trying to keep up with all the new techniques, equipment and buzzwords. New anglers are often intimidated and left wondering where to begin. People have been catching steelhead for hundreds of years and what worked then still works now. What could be simpler than fishing with a float, a few weights and piece of bait? I will throw a few common-sense observations your way and you will be fishing with the pros before you know it.

River Fishing Basics

Sometimes the most obvious things are overlooked. Here are a few basic hints about rods, reels, mainline, leaders and hooks.

A rod shorter than ten feet is generally inadequate for float fishing for steelhead because most West Coast rivers require long casts and long drifts to cover water. Small streams that only require short casts and short floats are the exception. Bait casting level wind reels are best able to cast lighter lines long distances and are favored by most steelhead fishermen. Center pin reels, or single-action reels are a favorite of ardent and longtime steelheaders but require a lot of patience and practice to master. Spinning reels are making a comeback with the availability of longer rods and the new spectra fishing lines. These lines float and do not stretch, which make it possible to float fish properly with a spinning reel set up. I prefer using a good level wind reel over the center pin reel because the level wind has a better and faster ability to cover water.

A river fisher's mainline should be between ten- and twenty-pound test. The most commonly used lines are twelve- and fifteen-pound test. Any mainline brand will do as long as it is a popular (and therefore proven) brand. Most tackle outlets carry only premium brands.

The leader strength chosen will be and should be dependent on the river conditions and size of the fish. As an example, a person fishing a fifteen-pound leader and twenty-pound mainline is set up for the largest rivers with the biggest fish. A person fishing an eight-pound leader and twelve-pound mainline is set up for medium-size rivers with small to medium fish.

The mainline should always be at least four to six pounds heavier in breaking strength than the leader. When an angler is losing lots of floats it usually means that the leader and mainline breaking strengths are too close together. If the mainline is fifteen pounds, the leader strength should be no more than ten pounds. A fisherman should always use a leader that will break when you need it to break. The leader strength is important. If a steelhead gets out of the control of the angler, the leader should break when the angler decides to put his thumb down on the spool and points the rod directly at the fish. This is especially true in places where the fish must be released unharmed. A forty-minute battle with a wild fish is not good news for the fish.

The leader strength and hook size are also correlated. It is important that the hook bends before the line breaks. For example, a #2 Gamagatzu hook bends before eight-pound test Maxima leader breaks. By knowing this relationship, it is not likely that a fish will break your line. The hook should almost always bend before the line breaks. The fish will generally come free before the line breaks. This in turn helps save a lot of tackle from ending up on the river bottom. With pliers and a file your hook is as good as new.

At this point I am assuming that the reader knows what a steelhead float is and what it looks like.

Not a day goes by in the winter when I see an angler fishing with a float incorrectly, or not using it to his or her full advantage.

As a general rule when fishing with a float, the longer the float length relative to the depth of the water, the fewer fish you catch. It doesn't mean any fewer bites. It only means you lose or miss more fish because of the delay between the bite and your hook set.

A properly fished float has the same or just slightly less distance between the float and the last or bottom weight, as compared to the depth of the river. A float should be fished straight up and down, with only a slight tilt toward the angler. When floats are fished shorter than the depth of the water, the hook ups are the best.

The steelhead has to come off the bottom to take the bait and when it does, the resistance from the float is immediate and the angler's hook set comes shortly after. The float going under is enough to keep a small, thin, chemically sharpened hook in the fish's mouth until you set the hook. In time you will start to notice that fish will never have the hooks in their gills or throats. This is because the first time the fish closes his month on the bait he gets hooked. The float pressure does not allow the fish any time to swallow the bait. Fishing a float that is longer than the depth of the water lets the fish have the bait for a longer moment before the float goes down. The fish has either more time to let it go or more time to swallow and each is bad news when fishing for steelhead.

Anyone who has spent time steelhead fishing is familiar with the old, "I got one...oh, he's gone." The float goes down, you strike and you get just enough of the fish to tell that it was a fish and not the bottom, again. If this is happening most of time when fishing steelhead, it means your float is too long.

When I am fishing and my float goes down, I put my thumb on the spool and hold back for a slight moment. If I feel a tug, I set the hook and if it is not a steelhead I continue my drift or try carefully to get my hook unstuck from the bottom. A hook set without a fish on the end is the best way I know to spook all the fish in the area. Trying to unstick a hook is the main action that keeps anglers from catching more fish in a single spot. Steelhead are very cautious by nature, and this is especially true in clear water. When something or someone enters their environment, they know it. Ripping a float through the water is like throwing rocks in the pool.

This brings us back to the long float. The longer the float, the more snags and ruckuses caused by your float. Getting hooked on the bottom once in a while is acceptable, but snags every second or third cast is a problem.

Fishing with Roe

Roe can be used with any weight method, but using split shot results in the best presentation. When fishing with split shot, the bottom shot should barely touch bottom, only once in a while. The bait is free to drift wherever the current takes it in the radius of the leader length.

Roe in a skein has some buoyancy and is easily pushed around by the current. This technique is suited for clear, walking-speed water. Remember—fish almost always feed looking up. In most cases the bait will be twelve to thirty inches from the bottom.

In fast or murky water heavier split shots and a little more contact with the bottom are required. The heavier weights make more contact with the bottom, which will hold back the bait and keep it close to the bottom. In fast or murky water the bait should be presented at eye level. This technique also works well in runs that have been heavily fished, or places where fish have been fished over and spooked and are reluctant to chase or move to their food (your bait).

Pencil lead is also good for keeping bait close to the bottom. Pencil lead with roe is a good combination for hard-to-catch fish and in places where the water is fast and there is a need to get your bait down in a hurry. When the lead hits the bottom, the bait is immediately forced down and out in front of the lead. The bait is in the strike zone on impact of the weight hitting the bottom. The weight of the pencil lead causes the bait to really slow down and unwilling fish get a good look at what you are offering. This can go both ways, some may bite, some will be scared off and some will actually just ignore it. As a general rule, most steelhead live in walking-speed water and the first technique using split shot is the method that I use for the majority of my fishing time.

A good rule if you are planning to fish a hole completely is to start shallow with small weights and work deeper with heavier weights.

Fishing with Sand Shrimp

Sand shrimp, unlike roe, are best fished with pencil lead and can be fished with or without a float. Sand shrimp are very light and buoyant, and easily tangle in the split shot on the cast or during the drift. It is generally a no-win situation, about which little can be done. A shrimp is best fished when it is forced down to the bottom by the heavier lead hitting the bottom. The shrimps' buoyancy and the fact that they are usually alive are what make them so appealing to fish. Steelhead will often have a hard time getting a good hold on the shrimp and will often try to pin it on the bottom. Small shrimp will actually shoot out of the fish's mouth when it tries to close down on the shrimp. A lot of steelhead are missed by anglers trying to set the hook on the first tug. If you strike too soon, it is easy to spook the fish, causing it to lose interest in your bait. It is better to let the fish tug a few times and in most cases the small hook will set itself in the corner of the fish's mouth. It takes a little practice to know when to set the hook. If the fish chews it too much there is greater risk of the fish swallowing the bait and damage occurring. This is especially true when not using a float. The float will pull back when the fish bites and generally the fish does not get hooked as deep in the mouth. With today's fine and chemically sharpened hooks, the resistance of the float being pulled under the water is enough to get the fish hooked.

Keeping sand shrimp alive

Shrimp work best when they are alive and healthy, and there are two techniques that have worked very well for me.

1) Place the shrimp in a large bucket of seawater. Every two days change the water and pick out the dead shrimp. It is possible to keep the shrimp alive for about ten days. This is

the best technique for long life, but having a fresh supply of seawater can be difficult for most people not living near the source.

2) Place the shrimp on or in dry, absorbent material; the material can be paper towel or wood chips. For better storage it is important to pick out the dead shrimp every day. A dead shrimp gives off a chemical that will kill the other shrimp. If the paper towel becomes damp, change it. Keep the shrimp refrigerated. Labeling the container in your fridge will help to avoid midnight-snacking accidents.

Fishing with Roe Bags

First of all, roe bags are single eggs in nylon mesh tied into a ball. Roe bags are best fished with split shot and a float. A roe bag is about the least buoyant of any natural bait.

The best way to fish a roe bag is with a long, light leader. In slower water the roe bag will sink quickly, dropping into the fish's view with no weights in sight. This has to be the best trick in the book.

Roe bags can be used without a float but tend to get stuck in the rocks. Small pieces of colored foam can be added in with the eggs to float them. It works, but it does take away from the natural egg appeal. You might be thinking that a floater, like a corky or spin-n-glow, will work—again, it will work, but looks a little funny.

I bottom bounce roe bags in places where there is gravel and not a lot of big rocks. These spots are very limited, so this technique gets very little use.

Roe bags can be attached to the hook two different ways. The first way is to hang the bag from the bottom of the hook so that the whole hook is exposed. Simply slide the hook under the knot that holds the bag together, making sure that you do not break any eggs. This method results in the best hook ups. When the fish bites the roe bag, he gets the hook at the same time. The fish never gets a chance to swallow the bait and hook. The first time the fish closes his mouth on the bait he is hooked.

The second way to attach a roe bag is by hanging it on the back of the hook using the roe loop to keep it in place. This allows the angler to add wool or other eye-catching materials. This method is best used in high or murky water when more color is needed to bring the fish to the bait.

Keep It Simple

I, too, have been a victim to the multifangled flangdangle that was supposed to revolutionize the way steelhead are caught. (I hope you are not disappointed that I have not talked about purple and black gadgets or yellow strawberry-flavored eggs—there is a reason for this.) Every year I try hard to catch fish on the latest and greatest lures and bait, and by December 15th I am back fishing the same baits and patterns that I have fished for the past ten years. Steelhead fishing is not about what is in your vest. In fact, the best fishermen I know can carry all the tackle they need in their right coat pocket.

Steelhead survive by eating natural bait, so it makes sense to fish with what steelhead like to eat.

When steelhead first poke their noses into fresh water, they eat the first semibuoyant object that passes by. This could be a piece of wood, plastic or rubber eggs. Steelhead are easy to trick the first couple of times, but after a few encounters they smarten up in a hurry.

Curing Fish Eggs for River Fishing

Chinook eggs

Chinook eggs should be cured as soon as possible once taken from the fish, as they tend to discolor very rapidly once they hit the air.

Standard commercial cures that can be bought in the store are the best. Most cures come with a coloring agent that will turn the eggs to any desired color. For chinook eggs, I buy the cures that turn the eggs bright red. If at all possible, the eggs should not be frozen before curing them. It is better to cure them and then put them in the freezer. The reason being, the outer eggs thaw before the center eggs. By the time the center of the skein is thawed the outer eggs will already have turned very dark. Eggs taken from less mature fish are better for

Artificial Baits

STEELHEAD WORMS: Size: ranges from 4 – 6 inches. **Color**: pale pink, bubble gum, hot pink, peach and white are popular. **Hook**: sizes range from #2 – #3/0 **Leader**: weight is 8 – 15 lb.; length is 16 – 36 in. <u>Note</u>: rigging the worm with a small salmon bead above the hook helps prevent the hook from tearing the worm.

JENSEN EGGS *(left and right)*
Sizes: small, medium and large pictured.
Color: orange, B.C. orange and cherise cheese are popular.

RIGGED SINGLE JENSEN EGGS
Eggs are rigged with a tuft of yarn.
Hook: sizes range from #4 – #1
Leader: weight is 6 – 10 lb.;
length is 24 –40 in.

JENSEN EGGS TIED IN SPAWN SACS
Hook: sizes range from #2 – #1/0
Leader: weight is 8 – 12 lb.;
length is 16 – 36 in.

GOOEY BOBS *(left and right)*
These baits are rigged with yarn and a salmon bead. **Size**: small, medium, large and magnum
pictured. **Color**: rocket red, B.C. orange, peach and pink are popular. **Hook**: sizes range from
#1/0 – #3/0. **Leader**: weight is 8–15 lb.; length is 16 – 36 in.

CORKIES These artificials are rigged with yarn.
Size: range from 6 – 14 in.
Color: orange, rocket red, peach and pink are popular.
Hook: sizes range from #2 – #1/0
Leader: weight is 6 – 12 lb.; length is 16 – 36 in.

YARN The yarn is rigged in two-tone contrasting colors.
Size: range from as small as a pea to the size of a quarter.
Basic Colors: peach, white, pink, orange, green chartreuse, red (over fifty different shades to choose from).
Hook: sizes range from #4 – #3/0
Leader: weight is 6 – 15 lb.; length is 16 – 40 in.
<u>Note</u>: Size and color used depends on water clarity and conditions.

SPIN 'N GLOWS *(left and right)*
These bait are rigged with and without yarn.
Size: range from 10 – 14. **Color**: pink, peach, orange, rocket red and purple are popular
Hook: sizes range from #2 – #3/0 **Leader**: weight is 6 – 12 lb.; length is 16 – 36 in.

Blades
Size: range from 1 – 5
Color: brass, copper, nickel, silver and gold in hammered or smooth finishes are popular
Hook: sizes range from #1 – #4/0
Leader: weight is 10 – 15 lb.; length is 16 – 36 in.

A wide range of steelhead hook sizes for every type of artificial or natural bait presentation. Shown, from left to right 1/0, 2/0, 3/0, 5/0, 4, 2, 1.

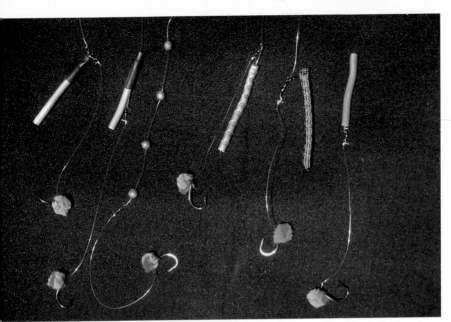

Six of the most popular West Coast weight systems for steelheading. Note that the leaders have been made Short for demonstration purposes only. Refer to Steve Kaye's chapter on artificial baits for correct leader lengths.

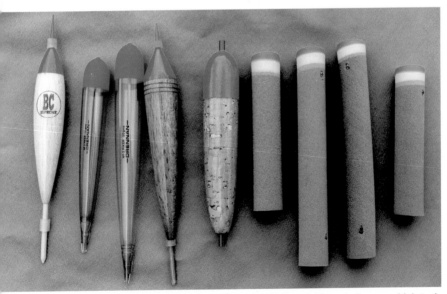

A wide selection of classic West Coast floats. Pictured from left to right are balsa, new high-tech plastics, wood, cork and inexpensive Styrofoam floats in a wide range of sizes. The size of the float used depends on the amount of weight beneath it. A good rule of thumb is to have no more than one inch of the float showing above water while making a drift through a run.

Author Steve Kaye about to land this 18 lb. male winter fish by drifting a sensitive drennan float between the fast and slow water for winter steelhead.

Above: A fine Skeena summer-run steelhead caught on a B.C. orange gooey bob.

Photo: Barry M. Thornton

Opposite: Author Steve Kaye releasing a prime winter steelhead from the Chilliwack River on a February afternoon.

Above: Mark Pendlington with a prime 16 lb male summer-run from the Thompson River. Never rule out spoons as a top producing artificial later in the season preferably when the river has some color from a fresh rain. This spoon is a three quarter ounce silver fireside croc by Gibbs.

Inset: A good selection of steelhead spoons in sizes ranging from ½ to 3 oz. in brass and silver.

Left: Rafts and driftboats for winter steelheading are quickly becoming the choice method for navigating West Coast rivers and a relaxing and enjoyable way to spend a day.

Author Steve Kaye and Mark Pendlington admire the colors of this 18 lb. male Chilliwack winter steelhead.It doesn't get any better than this.

Above right and below: Pontoon boats are for experienced winter steelheaders with a good life insurance policy, but they do get you to the water that the crowds don't see. Courses on pontoon rafting are available at most whitewater rafting companies and are highly recommended.

Natural Baits

CURED ROE *(left and right)*
These are cured and boraxed hatchery steelhead roe, cut to size and ready for use.
Color: they have a natural peach-pink color.

Left: **PRERIGGED LEADER BOARD**
David Murphy's prerigged leader board shows numerous examples of three eggs tied on the shank of a hook. The ones pictured are Jensen eggs.
Size: pictured below in hand.
Color: orange and peach.
Hook: sizes range from #2–2/0.

Below: **ROE HOLDER**
Chemically sharpened octopus hook is rigged with custom jensen egg and yarn awaiting hatchery steelhead roe.

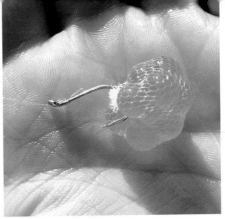

FINISHED ROE AND JENSEN COMBO

David Murphy's tried and tested Jensen egg and roe combination.

Size: 1–2 inches in diameter.
Color: peach-pink color
Hook: sizes range from #2–2/0.

RIGGED SPAWN SAC

Individual salmon eggs are tied in a spawn sac mesh.

Size: ranges from 1–1/0.
Color: natural peach-pink color
Hook: sizes range from #4–#1/0
Leader: weight is 6–10 lb.; length is 16–36 in.
<u>Note</u>: See how the hook is rigged through the spawn sac knot? This allows a much better hook-up ratio.

Author and guide David Murphy navigates class 3 whitewater backwards to get down from a steelhead run. It shows the skills required to be a guide on some of the West Coast rivers.

A crisp November morning produces this magnificent Thompson River doe working a Gibbs iron-head one ounce spoon across the river by sweeping and tapping bottom the entire way.

Above: Roe sacs for steelhead can't be beat for winter fish.

Below: Center pin reels and steelhead—a West Coast tradition.

Tony Awesome and David Murphy showing the reward of a day's winter steelheading on the Stamp River in Port Alberni, British Columbia where David guides.

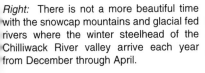

Above: Barry Thornton holds a large silver-bright Vancouver Island winter steelhead.
Photo: Barry M. Thornton

Right: There is not a more beautiful time with the snowcap mountains and glacial fed rivers where the winter steelhead of the Chilliwack River valley arrive each year from December through April.

Plugs

Some of Matt Guiguet's personal plug collection—Jensen Hot Shots in sizes 25–65. Colors ranging from silver, metallic, gold, green and blue, with or without rattles. Note the swivel between the Siwash hook and plug body. Single barbless hooks are mandatory on West Coast rivers.

Left: Notice the fast-change clip on this plug that allows for the quick change of color and size of plug without retying each time.

Below: The author's full selection of plugs he takes with him on a day's plug pulling for steelhead.

These faces focus on what is ahead—class 5 whitewater between steelhead runs on this river. There is a two thousand foot elevation drop over twenty kilometers of this river where Matt guides on Vancouver Island.

Precise driftboat control and carefully tuned plugs are essential for success. Working the run from top to bottom and side to side.

Right: Watching the vibrations of the rod tips and checking that the lines are fishing exactly the same distance behind the boat.

Below: A well equipped drift boat for the ultimate West Coast steelheading experience.

can be a waiting game at times. Not all of a river"s steelhead runs are productive waters. The aggressive fish may hold in two of the ten runs you may choose to fish that day.

20 lb. male winter fish is about to be landed from a Vancouver Island river using a #35 gold ot shot.

The reward for a successful day of plug pulling.

Not all water is plug water. Have other rods rigged and ready for various fishing conditions.

Here Matt puts a quarter ounce marabou jig through a likely looking steelhead run. Simply adjust float to the desired depth and fish the run. The spinning reel allows for a drag-free drift through the run whereby the float and the jig are always straight up and down.

Male steelhead readily attack plugs because they are territorial.

Matt Guiguet with the telltale smile after a good day's steelheading.

Opposite: Mark plays a Gold River plug-caught steelhead. The final few minutes of the day at the end of the drift provided the opportunity to bring this male steelhead to hand. It pays to fish a steelhead run to the end of the day!

Art Lingren's Steelhead Fly Patterns

GENERAL PRACTITIONER (ORANGE)
Hook: #2 – 5/0 low-water salmon
Tail: orange polar bear hair, red-gold pheasant breast feather
Body: orange wool or seal fur
Eyes: golden pheasant tippet feather
Rib: medium, oval, gold tinsel
Hackle: orange cock neck feather
Wing: golden pheasant breast feathers with overwing of orange-red hen neck feather
Head: black cellire varnish

GENERAL PRACTITIONER (BLACK)
Hook: #2 – 5/0 low-water salmon
Tail: black squirrel tail, red-gold pheasant breast feather
Body: wrap hook shank with lead then black mohair or wool
Eyes: golden pheasant tippet feather
Rib: medium, oval, silver tinsel
Hackle: black cock neck feather
Wing: black spade hackles, larger black wood duck or black hen neck feathers
Head: black cellire varnish

SQUAMISH POACHER
Hook: #2
Tail: sparse orange bucktail
Eyes: green glass
Body: fluorescent orange chenille
Rib: silver or copper wire or fluorescent red-orange thread
Hackle: orange
Wing: fluorescent orange surveyor's tape carapace

STEELHEAD BEE
Hook: #2 – #10
Tail: fox squirrel, quite bushy
Body: equal sections of dark brown, yellow brown wool, silk or seal fur
Hackle: natural brown, ginger or honey, sparse
Wing: fox squirrel, quite bushy, set slightly forward and well divided

BOMBER

Hook: #2 – #6 Wilson dry-fly salmon
Tail: deer hair—natural or other colors
Body: deer hair clipped cigar shaped
Rib: none
Hackle: fly tyer's fancy
Optional Wing: deer hair protruding over eye of hook

DOC SPRATLEY

Hook: #1 – #4 low-water salmon
Tip: fine, oval silver tinsel
Tag: fluorescent green floss
Tail: a few sprigs of guinea fowl
Butt: black ostrich herl
Body: black floss and seal fur with black hackle over front half
Rib: silver oval tinsel
Throat: Guinea fowl
Wing: slender strips of center tail feather from the ring-necked pheasant
Head: Peacock herl

TAYLOR'S GOLDEN SPEY

Hook: #4 – #5/0 low-water salmon
Body: rear one half of hot orange floss and front half of hot orange seal fur
Rib: flat silver tinsel followed by medium, oval tinsel
Hackle: gray heron feather
Throat: golden pheasant red-orange breast feather or lemon wood duck flank feather
Wing: two golden pheasant red-orange breast feather

BLACK SPEY

Hook: #2 – #6 Wilson dry-fly salmon
Tip: fine oval, gold tinsel
Butt: black floss
Tail: red-orange Indian crow-type feather
Body: black floss
Rib: medium or fine gold twist to match hook size
Hackle: black heron or lawful substitute
Throat: teal flank feather
Wing: bronze mallard
Head: black cellire varnish

WOOLLY WORM
Hook: #2/0 – #10 regular salmon
Tail: short tuft of red or orange wool
Body: black chenille
Hackle: grizzly

COWICHAN SPECIAL
Hook: #10 – #4
Tail: a few sprigs from a white hackle
Body: red or orange chenille
Collar: soft, white hackle

COMBO BUG
Hook: #4 or #6 Tiemco TMC 200
Tail: deer hair or none
Body: black foam
Rib: black rod-binding thread
Wing & Throat: deer hair
Collar: deer hair ends

AS SPECIFIED NO. 1 & 2
Hook: #2 – #10 low-water salmon
Tip: fine, gold, oval tinsel
Tag: purple floss
Tail: purple hackle feather
Body: purple floss with purple seal fur
Rib: medium, gold, oval tinsel
Hackel: black hackle feather with one side stripped to maintain sparseness
Throat: teal or widgeon flank feather with one side stripped
Wing: bronze mallard (No. 1), black squirrel (No. 2)
Head: black cellire varnish

Above: Peter Caverhill releasing a wild Dean River summer-run.

Left: When the desire is strong, the winter steelhead er will fish in all kinds of weather including fog, rain and snow.

Below: A big Thompson River buck steelhead taken on a Black GP. The Thompson River steelhead are some of the hardest fishing steelhead in the world.

Previous page: Michael Uehara takes a rest while Gary Baker fishes for Squamish River winter-runs on an April day.

Opposite: The shaded parts of a river are far more productive those which are sunlit.

Photos: Art Lingren

A selection of flies to suit the five presentations. *Photo: Art Lingren*

Right: When the river flows colored and steelhead are running a big fly may be the answer.
Photo: Art Lingren

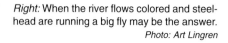

When the river flows with glacial melt and steelhead are moving there is a chance to take a steelhead even on bright sunny days. *Photo: Art Lingren*

Rob Brown, the Skeena Angler, fishing the mighty Skeena.   *Photo: Art Lingren*

Steelhead flies and tying materials with Art Lingren writing in the background.   *Photo: Art Lingren*

Above: Fall with its misty and frosty morning is a great time to be drifting a summer-run river like the Bulkley. *Photo: Art Lingren*

Left: This fall steelhead took Art Lingren Black Caterpillar Bomber pattern in a show rise. *Photo: Art Lingren*

Below: A black bear searching for salmon cacasses while a fly fisher probes the depths the Thompson's Y Run. *Photo: Art Lingren*

steelhead than eggs taken closer to spawning because the eggs from a less mature fish have more membrane connecting the eggs, which allows them to stay on the hook better.

Chinook egg recipe

Using scissors, cut the eggs into usable bait-size pieces (about the size of a one-dollar coin). The eggs are formed in layers and it is possible to break very few eggs during this process.

Place eggs into liquid dye or colored bait cure for ten to twenty minutes.

Strain the liquid from the eggs and let the eggs stand in the strainer for ten minutes (a powdered dry cure will also form a lot of liquid, which must be drained). The liquid can now be used again but the soak time will be about double.

Place the eggs on absorbent material on a fine screen. Let them dry for ten to twenty hours or until they're dry and tacky. The drier the better.

Mix the dry pieces with 20 Mule Team Borax soap. The borax absorbs any left over moisture and cures the membrane, which holds the eggs together. The borax is ultimately responsible for keeping the eggs on your hook.

The eggs are now ready to be used or put into an airtight container and frozen.

When freezing eggs, be sure that the eggs are completely covered in borax. This helps to stop the eggs from oxidizing and going bad.

Chum eggs

Chum eggs are the most readily available eggs for river fishermen. Almost all tackle and bait shops in the Pacific Northwest have a good supply in the months of October and November. The eggs are taken as seconds from the commercial chum fishery. The chum salmon is most valued for the roe, with 99 percent going to the raw fish market. The leftovers that are not up to par for eating go to the bait shops. Chum eggs are pale in color and are best cured with a red or orange coloring cure. These eggs are very durable and last a long time before going bad if left out—perfect for bait shop refrigerators.

Chum egg recipe

With scissors, cut the roe into bait-size pieces. Mix with powered or liquid red coloring cure—a little bait cure goes a long way.

Let stand in the bait cure for ten to twenty minutes.

Strain the liquid from the eggs. This can take a while.

Place on absorbent material or screen for ten to twenty hours. It is a good idea to do this outside. The drying time will depend on the humidity of the air.

When dry to the touch, mix the eggs with ample amounts of 20 Mule Team Borax soap.

Place the eggs in a sealed container and freeze until your next steelhead trip.

Coho eggs

Coho eggs are generally the most available eggs and the easiest to cure for the river angler. In most cases the eggs are red, small and resemble steelhead eggs. Coho eggs are durable and do not need as immediate attention as chinook eggs. If a couple of days go by, the eggs will still have their color and will cure up very well.

Coho egg recipe

Using scissors, cut eggs into bait-size pieces. Place on absorbent material for approximately one hour.

Place the eggs in a bowl or on newspaper. Add ample amounts of borax and mix thoroughly with your hands. After this process, the eggs will be dry to the touch. The eggs are now ready to be used or frozen in an airtight container.

Coho eggs do not change color when cured with a coloring cure. The eggs will just turn a darker shade of red. As a general rule, the lighter the eggs are in color the better a colored cure will work.

Steelhead eggs

Steelhead eggs are the ultimate bait for catching steelhead. These eggs will stay on the hook better than any other egg. They do not lose their color as fast as other eggs, which makes a little bait go a long way. Unfortunately, they are very hard to obtain, as only hatchery steelhead are allowed to be retained.

Steelhead egg recipe
Using scissors, cut eggs into bait-size pieces. Place on paper or in a bowl and add ample amounts of 20 Mule Team Borax. Mix thoroughly until the eggs are dry to the touch (drying the eggs first is not necessary). Use within a week or freeze.

Steelhead eggs freeze better than any other eggs. The eggs will look and fish just as well as the fresh eggs.

There are hundreds of different ways to cure eggs and from my experience, the easier the better. I am fishing most days of the season and the less time I have to spend preparing my bait the better. I have used the same curing techniques for the past fifteen years. New products come out every year to help make curing bait easier, but the basic principles will always be the same.

My steelhead techniques have been carved to fit my needs for the conditions and rivers that I fish. Most rivers and steelhead have similar traits but exceptions exist in every river. Time on the water will relinquish these exceptions and help you establish your own simple techniques. After a lifetime of guiding I have come to realize and accept that in a day's fishing I cannot catch every fish in the river. For every five that I catch there were twenty or thirty that I did not. What keeps me going, is that out of that twenty or thirty that I did not catch, five might bite tomorrow.

lanforbes

Plug Fishing for Steelhead

by Matt Guiguet

Plug fishing for steelhead started sometime in the mid to late fifties in Oregon and northwestern California. The plug of choice then was the Eddie Pope & Co. "Hot Shot."

During this time the world of fishing was being revolutionized with new technology. Fishing rods made from bamboo were being replaced with fiberglass, the drift boat design was being refined from a basic dory into an easily maneuverable rowboat, and the invention of monofilament fishing line made "cutty hunk" line obsolete. At the same time the original wind reels were being introduced by Ambassador.

Plugs were either fished from a boat or cast from shore. Rivers in which this technique was pioneered include the Rogue, Klamath and Clackamas Rivers. The slick maneuverability of the drift boat and the ability to "back troll" (row against the current) made fishing with plugs a very effective way to entice big steelhead to bite.

There are many ways to fish plugs for steelhead and salmon, including casting from shore, fishing from jet boats or using side planers. My experiences have been angling with plugs for steelhead from a boat on Vancouver Island rivers. I will therefore concentrate on plug fishing from a drift boat, since this is from where my learning and experiences have been gleaned. Plugs don't just catch steelhead. Over the years I have had many incidental catches of coho, chinook, chum, brown trout and cutthroat trout, but once again I will keep the focus on winter steelhead.

I enjoy fishing plugs for a number of reasons, plugs provide a good method for finding fish and new holding waters, they cover a lot of water faster and more efficiently than other methods, and are great for novice to advanced anglers. Plugs also allow anglers the opportunity to enjoy more views and scenery along the river instead of being always intensely focused on the cast or drift.

As I mentioned, one great thing about plug fishing is that just about anyone with any level of experience can catch a steelhead on a plug. Back trolling with plugs is a great and effective way to catch steelhead without all the frustration of constant backlashes and loosing gear on the bottom or in the trees.

Plug fishing for steelhead in B.C. isn't as popular or practiced as much as it is in the United States. As a result, the variety of color, sizes and types of steelhead plugs available to the angler has been limited. The only plugs that I have seen readily available and that work very well are the Luhr Jensen Hot Shot series.

Why Fish Bite Plugs

Steelhead are attracted to and bite plugs for two main reasons. The first reason they bite is that the plug resembles food. When steelhead first enter the river system from the ocean, they are still the same animals that have been feeding daily in order to survive. From the time it emerged from the gravel as a fry to the last day it spent in the ocean, feed, feed, feed.... Therefore, the instinct to bite something, especially during the times they like to bite, such as daylight hours and tide changes, is still there. So anything that fits into a steelhead's prey profile becomes potential food, including the back-trolled plug.

The other reason that steelhead bite plugs is that when steelhead get into the river they become very territorial. I find this particularly true with large male steelhead. When a properly fished plug comes swimming down right in front of a steelhead that has staked his claim to that small piece of water, the fish will try to scare off any competing intruders. So if that intruder includes the back-trolled plug, you are in for a lot of excitement.

How Fish Approach the Plug

When you back troll plugs down through a run and there are fish in it, there are a number of things that can happen, but for sure, you are going to move the fish.

1. They are going to hammer one of the plugs.

2. They are going to avoid your plugs, move around them and your boat and either move to a different part of the pool or downstream.

3. They will back down slowly to the tailout of the run in an effort to avoid the plugs, this is where most of the bites happen. The fish have moved down as you have trolled down, at this point they either strike really hard, or take off downstream so fast you'll never know these ghosts were even there.

The steelhead's behavior is what intrigues me most. The more I fish for them the more intriguing I find them. There have been numerous occasions over the years when I have just finished plugging a run and figured, "Oh well, I guess there wasn't anybody home there today," or some other fishing guide excuse. Then I look behind me and see an angler approach the run and make a cast and nail a beautiful fish that proceeds to put on a spectacular fight, jumping and running, a big performance for my jealous clients. What I am getting at is that sometimes going over top of the fish and moving them will change their "mood" and put them into a biting mode, even though they hadn't been interested earlier.

I am in no way promoting rowing back and forth over stacked up fish or herding them around or throwing rocks into pools. In the natural course of a drift down the river you will go over top of fish and they will move, to the advantage of both the shore fisherman and the drifters.

Steelhead react, the big trick is to get them to react positively to your gear, be it plugs, flies, bait or spinners. One of the negative reactions I have seen is when they will just watch your gear drift right by their nose time and time again. Or you'll cast upstream of the fish and you see your gear drifting toward the steelhead, and as soon as he sees it he hightails it downstream right out of the pool and you even think he's going back to the ocean. This situation is not a confidence builder, but really there are a lot of other factors involved in this. Water temperature and clarity both play huge roles in how a fish will react to a plug. Remember that fish are cold blooded and their metabolism is affected by even as much a one-degree water temperature fluctuation. Another factor affecting steelhead is that after spending so much time in the ocean with vast amounts of water around them, coming into the realm of a river with colder water and very limited space is quite a change. So one can expect a very skittish and spooky temperament.

Plug Fishing from a Drift Boat

Fishing plugs from a boat requires very little basic gear, a couple of rod holders and plug rods and reels and you are set. You should mount your rod holders at the same position on both sides of the boat. This will result in your rod tips lining up in the exact same horizontal positions on each side of the boat, so that your plugs are out the same distance behind the boat. The reason you want your plugs out the same distance is that they will work as a "team" going down the river. If one plug is ahead of the other plug, the steelhead may avoid one and move between the two and then avoid the other and has now virtually "escaped" your lures. The concept of the team is that they create an aggravating wall to the steelhead. This aggravation may entice the strike, if not, the wall may push them downstream while still facing your plugs, which still offers the chance of a strike.

I generally trail my plugs forty to sixty feet behind the boat to maintain the best control of the plugs. And as I mentioned, I like my plugs to fish side by side. If one is out farther than the other they are not fishing as effectively as they could. To achieve this balance, simply count out the number of pulls from the reel to the first eye on the rod, or count how many times your level wind goes across your reel.

Once your plugs are out, you can check their locations by looking at the angle of the line where it goes into the water. If it is the same of each side, you are all set. Ideally you want to be getting your gear into the water while you are anchored. This is also the best time to check that your plugs are tuned (covered later in the chapter) and fishing correctly.

When back trolling the plugs, start at the very top of the pool and begin to work your way downstream, working side to side trying to keep the plugs within the areas of the run where you think the fish are. Working the plugs this way is very effective because you can cover almost the whole run in a relatively short period of time. On certain runs I fish, I will sometimes slide back and forth across one section of river two or three times before moving downstream. This is especially effective if I have caught steelhead in this spot on previous trips.

When you have reached the bottom of the pool and the fish are now in the tailout, this is where the fish now usually makes one of two choices. It either hits the plug that has been closing in—and hits it hard—or it takes off as fast as it can. Quite often the strike zone is on the "lip" of the tailout. Always work the tailouts completely before leaving the run and heading downstream to the next place.

The Strike

One of the most exciting things to see is the awesome take of a steelhead on a plug. It is a bone-jarring violent hit that literally doubles the rod over and sends an adrenaline rush like no other strike I have experienced. When this happens, it is very important for the oarsman to row upstream as hard and fast as he can to keep tension on the line while the angler does his or her best to get the rod out of the holder and hang onto the fish. It is best to try to move the boat in close to shore and anchor in a good spot to land the fish.

There are some exceptions to the way steelhead will take a plug. Sometimes there will be a slight hesitation in the rod tip action, this is because the fish hit the plug and missed it and quite often will come right back and hammer the plug. I have seen fish hit so hard and fast that the rod is still in the rod holder and pointing downstream with the line just peeling off, but the fish is in the air beside the boat and heading upstream. That is the kind of excitement that makes all this rowing worthwhile.

When to and When Not to Plug Fish

I generally don't start fishing a run with plugs until I have fished the run with drift gear first (with the idea of using a finesse presentation so I don't spook the fish with the plugs). The reason for this is that you are giving the fish the opportunity to take a naturally drifted bait or lure first if the fish are in a feeding-biting mode. This gives us the chance to get a couple fish with drift gear. Then after you feel the fish that remain are not interested, proceed to fish plugs to work on their territorial instinct aspect of attraction.

On days when the river you are fishing is crowded and there have been a few boats ahead of you, this is the prime time for fishing plugs for most of the day. Normally the anglers ahead of you have fished the runs with drift gear. By fishing plugs behind them, you are showing the fish something they haven't seen yet. This strategy can often raise strikes even in heavily fished pools.

New Rivers

When you start to fish a new river, pulling plugs is a good way to find where the good holding spots are for fish. Every river is different in where the fish like to lie. When you are back trolling plugs, your lure is in the water all the time. You will eventually learn where the fish hold in a particular river in different river conditions, including clarity, water levels and even overcast versus sunny days. Soon you will know which water to skip over and where your effort should be concentrated, thereby creating your own hot spots and utilizing your time efficiently and effectively. This type of learning curve does not happen overnight—it is still happening for me every day I am on the river. Keeping a log book is a great way to compile this type of information. What you thought was just a lucky bite indeed may have some pattern and reasoning behind it. Record the level of the water, time of year, moon phase, color of plug, water temperature and whatever else you may find relevant. In a couple of steelhead seasons you will see how invaluable this information becomes.

Drift Boat Safety

Fishing plugs from a drift boat requires some basic equipment and knowledge about river fishing and navigating a boat down a river. If you have never rowed a boat down a river, don't start in the middle of winter steelhead season. Hire a guide for the first few times, and practice in the summer in medium water conditions when water temperatures and wave action are not severe. Practice on the river you intend to winter fish, so you get to know where the big rocks are and gain the local knowledge that is necessary for high water conditions. After you have achieved a level of confidence in medium water conditions, you'll be better at reading the river from an oarsman's perspective.

I have seen a few mishaps on the Cowichan River and heard of several more situations where inexperienced anglers have bought a boat and have attempted to drift with no prior experience in rowing or river rafting. On one occasion the boat and all the equipment were lost; luckily for the anglers, they made it to shore. There have been other accidents in which the occupants were not so fortunate.

Plug Sizes

The Hot Shot plug is available in four sizes that work well for steelhead. Plugs #25 and #35 are the type that rattle. The #30 and #40 series are the nonrattle design. The plugs I use the most are #35, #30 and #25. In most of the different river conditions I encounter over the winter fishing on Vancouver Island, all of these will fit the bill.

The #25 is the largest of my favorite three; it is ideal for high-water conditions or when visibility is limited. The rattle makes up for what the fish can't see and they find this attractive. I only keep a couple of these with me in the boat since they are my least-used plugs.

The #35 plug is probably the most versatile size in the Hot Shot series. It has a broad diving bill that will take it down to fifteen feet with the right amount of current and rowing. These plugs come with rattles in them, which seems to enhance their attractability. Under low clear water or bright light conditions these rattles seem to put the fish off, so I do not recommend them for these types of conditions. This plug does fish well in most winter conditions.

The #30 is a little smaller than the #35 and has no rattle in it. The diving bill is also narrower than the #35. This plug dives to about ten feet when the water is low and clear. I find that this plug is the one to use if the fish are a little spooky.

Learning which size to use is easy after a few drifts and reading the water. I always carry good numbers of these sizes, since river conditions can change in just a few short hours.

Plug Colors

Matching plug colors to river conditions is just as important as plug size. There are some basic rules to follow. However, since every river is different, each has its own definition of good visibility and low visibility. An example would be the Cowichan River—a good day can be called clear for the Cowichan, yet by comparison this visibility may be described as poor if the fisher has experience on the Stamp or Gold Rivers. So we have to keep in mind that conditions on one river, may not necessarily apply to another.

Fishing a small coastal stream with clear water and low to medium flows using a #25 fluorescent red Hot Shot with rattles would probably scare every fish it encounters back to the safety of the ocean. In low, clear situations I would try a #30 with one of the metallic finishes. An example of this being a #30 Blue Pirate—a classic plug for these conditions.

The most popular colors of Hot Shot plugs are the metallic blue, green-gold, gold, pink, blue, green and red. There are many, many more colors and color combinations but the ones listed above are basic and work. A good rule of thumb is bright plugs in murk low visibility water and darker plugs in clear water. If the river you are fishing has a greenish tinge to it, then you want to pick a darker plug that would look natural in it, so a plug closer to green would be the one to choose. If you were to fish a river that was gin clear, a silver or silver-blue would be the one of choice.

Tuning Plugs

You will have noticed that previously I referred to "tuning" plugs. By tuning I mean the process whereby one adjusts the Hot Shot eye and hook eye so that the lure action results in the lure running straight. This is the first thing I do when I pull a new plug out of the box, after I play a fish or even if I snag it on bottom. It doesn't take much to throw a plug out of balance. Tune and re-tune!

All Hot Shots come with a snap attached to the eye of the plug. This is where you attach your line. The round eye, to which this snap is attached, is a screw. This screw eye goes into the bill of the plug. This eye must be lined up properly with the bill of your plug or your plug will not swim. To start the tuning process this eye screw should be parallel with the sides of the plug bill.

You must be on the water to do this exercise. Pull the plug upstream and observe how it swims through the water, if it is veering off to one side or the other it needs to be adjusted. You want the plug to dive straight down. To fix this you need a pair of needlenose pliers and a little bit of experimenting with changing the angle of the eye screw. The general rule is, if the plug runs slightly to the left, adjust the round eye screw to the right. Use caution not to over adjust. If the plug pulls to the right, then adjust the eye screw to the left. This takes a little bit of fiddling around at first, but after a while you get good at it.

A plug that is out of tune will not dive straight down. It will dive off to the side and eventually flip up to the surface on the troll. When this happens to a good plug, it just means it's time to re-tune. Some plugs will outfish others and other plugs just will not fish. Get rid of these, remove them from your tackle box—they make a great key chain float.

Rods and Reels for Plug Fishing

My rod of choice for plugging is an eight and a half foot, medium-action rod designed for eight- to twelve-pound test line rated for 3/8-oz. to 3/4-oz. lures. This rod has a sensitive tip, which is very important because it is a visual aid to monitor how your plug is behaving. This rod also has enough backbone to land fish in the twenty-pound range and be able to handle the intensity of the steelhead strike. If a rod is too light, it will just bend and not set the hook, and if it is too stiff you won't be able to read the tip at all. Underpowered rods are hard on fish because it takes too long to land them and you don't get many solid hook ups.

I usually carry six to eight drift and spinning rods with me in the boat on a trip so that I can be prepared for various water conditions, including some that are shorter than my drift rods which helps with the space problem in a drift boat. Another advantage to the shorter rods is that they allow you to work your boat close to or under hanging branches or close to shore. Keep in mind that other than length, the rods should be identical. This is important when you are watching your rod tip action, because they will portray the same action and it is then easier to understand what is going on. A mixed pair of rods is much harder to work with and read correctly. A mixed pair also makes it difficult to make sure your plugs are out the same distance.

Choosing the right reel for plugging is also important. A level wind reel with a very smooth drag system combined with line capacity is what I look for. Look for a reel with a capacity of 250 yards of twelve-pound test line. There is really no need to cast plugs when fishing from a boat, so single-action reels are fine. Reels with the clicker option are nice to fish with because they provide an audio alarm for strike detection.

Fishing Line

Over the years I have tried many different makes and styles of lines, and I have found I prefer twelve-pound test clear or green monofilament. Green seems to work best in most conditions. When the water is low and clear and I am using the smaller-sized plugs, I will sometimes attach a six- to eight-foot leader of ten-pound using a small barrel swivel as my connection.

I have tried some of the high visibility lines and they work well for making sure your plugs are out the same distance. If you choose to fish with these, make sure you use a six- to eight-foot leader of clear or green monofilament between your plug and your mainline.

Monofilament lines ranging from ten- to fifteen-pound test all work plugs effectively. Using line lighter than ten-pound test runs the risk of it breaking off right at the onset of the strike. Using too heavy a mainline will detract from the swimming action of the plugs.

When choosing a line, it is important to get the best quality possible. A line with good abrasion resistance, low visibility under water, good knot strength and low memory will all make your plug fishing more successful.

Rigging Plugs for Fishing

When you buy a plug it generally comes right out of the box with a large siwash hook or a treble hook. Conservation and regulations have dictated that treble hooks are not allowed for plug pulling on West Coast rivers. The single siwash hook that comes with the plug is too big and can do severe damage to steelhead, something we all want to avoid. I prefer to remove the original hook and put a small split ring on the hook tow eye, then I add a #12 barrel swivel then another small split ring before finally putting on a 1/0 bait style hook. This is important because it places the hook at the right distance behind the plug to achieve maximum hook ups. The smaller hook will not penetrate deeply enough to mortally wound a steelhead. These smaller hooks get the fish in the lips or nose every time. And this hook set up is plenty strong enough to get a twenty-pound-plus steelhead to the boat without straightening out the rigging.

The swivel in this set up allows the hook to spin freely off the plug, so when you are fighting a steelhead and he starts twisting, he is not twisting against the plug. When the plug is rigged straight to the hook, the plug can actually lever the hook out of the fish's mouth. This swivel also gets to hook further away from the plug; so when the fish bites, it gets hooked, instead of having the plug bounce out of its mouth.

The ethical problem of causing damage from the use of oversized hooks is easily overcome by using smaller hooks in every application of our fishing, including spoons, spinners, baits and flies. This is great for the fish and the angler. I highly recommend it.

Attach your leader to the snap that comes attached to the plug's tow eye. This snap allows the plug to swim freely on it, whereas if you were to attach the line directly to the tow eye, the plug's action would be impeded. If you intend to run your mainline straight to the snap, there is no need to have a swivel somewhere in between since these plugs do not rotate or spin. This clip also makes changing plugs really easy since they just snap onto the next plug you intend to fish.

Ethics

When I started drift boat fishing there were relatively few other boats fishing, even on a busy day on the Cowichan River. I may have seen two boats all day and usually knew the other anglers. Over the last few years, river fishing for winter steelhead has become more and more popular and this trend is not changing. There is a variety of methods, techniques and preferences. They all have to be respected, which means we all have to give a little space or movement to avoid unnecessary tension. If you are drifting in a boat, conduct yourself in a manner that gives space to anglers on shore. Usually plain, old common sense prevails. Three rules of thumb are:

1. Don't drop your anchor where other anglers are trying to fish.
2. Don't pull plugs through a run where bank anglers are already fishing.
3. Be courteous and congenial with your fellow anglers.

Steelhead fishing is more personal than other types of fishing. And I think it is this feeling that creates the animosity or tension between the different gear user types. No one gear preference has the right to dictate to others how, when, where or why they should fish. British Columbia is a world class fisherman's paradise that is open to the public for only the cost of a fishing license. Let us work together to keep it that way.

Ian Forbes

Fly Fishing for Winter and Summer Steelhead

by Art Lingren

Wow, what a fish!

Severely shaken by the rush of adrenaline as I knelt down to take the hook from the steelhead's mouth, those few words inadequately describe what had transpired over the previous few minutes. I love to fly fish for summer-run steelhead, and I love to bring the fish up to the surface to take a surface- or just-under-the-surface-presented fly. On this trip I had been at the fabled Dean River, located along B.C.'s central coast in Fisheries Management Region 5, for six days. Today I thought I would walk up to the Fir Pool. I couldn't leave the Dean without fishing the pool where I took my first summer-run steelhead fifteen seasons earlier. I had heard great changes had altered the pool, and although the changes to the Fir Pool were drastic, they didn't surprise me. I have wandered too many rivers over the past thirty-plus years and few, if any, have been unchanged by water flow—one of nature's most fascinating and powerful forces.

A large gravel bar had developed diagonally from the tail of the Fir to the bottom of the chute flowing from the upstream Grizzly Run. It looked wadeable. It was, and I could fish the classic fish-holding gut—a spot in a river that will stop a fish from migrating further upriver because of its depth and velocity—that had developed near the left bank. (The best spot turned out to be a little further downstream from where I started, but one should cover all likely looking water. Sometimes you don't know what the water will fish like until you do a drift or two.) By methodically working the water I intended to work my way through the gut and was just enjoying being alive and on the Dean. I have caught steelhead from thirty-six of British Columbia's rivers through the years, but

80

this day a fish took my Black Spey fly so violently and put up such a struggle, taking me well into my backing line, it had me scurrying over the rocks like never before. This thirty-three-inch male was truly one of the best fish I have ever caught. Perhaps the fish of a lifetime, but I will continue to cast my flies on steelhead waters hoping that someday a better fish will find my flies as attractive as this fish. Such are the dreams of steelhead fly fishers.

Steelhead Trout

What an unusual handle: steelhead. I have often wondered about the name's origin and spent nine months one year writing to museums and researching fisheries papers. Eventually I found early written records that showed steelhead and hardhead were the common names adopted by coastal market fishermen for this fish in the 1870s and perhaps earlier.

The steelhead is a seagoing rainbow trout. It spawns and offspring rear from one to three or four years in freshwater, depending on available food and growing season, before migrating to the ocean where they grow to a large size. When the steelhead returns to the river, it has a steely blue dorsal surface, silvery sides with black spots on its back, dorsal fin and tail. As it continues to mature after entering freshwater, it takes on the telltale coloration of its rainbow ancestors. Females, after months in freshwater, may only show a slight tinge of pink on the cheeks and have a light rainbow hue along the lateral line. Males color much more and more quickly. Steelhead return to fresh water to spawn after spending from a few months to three years ocean-feeding, and can range in size from about two pounds to more than thirty pounds. Although steelhead vary greatly in size, a five-pound steelhead is a small fish in British Columbia and any fish fifteen pounds and larger is a good-sized fish in most rivers.

Taking Times

When the steelhead makes its return to the river, it may hold near the mouth of the river until water conditions suit migration. On large rivers, like the Fraser and Skeena, that have large flows even at low levels, upstream migrations are not hampered. On some of the coastal rivers, the run is drawn in by an increase in flow, and on many rivers migration is instigated by the spring runoff.

Fast-running steelhead are poor "takers." However, a freshly arrived steelhead as it moves slowly up-river, stopping here and there to test the current, is an alert fish and can be a grand taker. Providing the angler matches his method to water conditions, the fish are relatively easy to catch. This is the time when inexperienced anglers often have good sport and experienced anglers have better sport.

After the run has arrived and the fish settle in, the fishing can vary from great to lousy, and success or failure is dependent on being there at the right time and the fish being undisturbed. On rivers popular with weekend fishers, Saturday can often be much better than Sunday. But, there are times after a run when water conditions change, and existing fish that have been difficult to catch suddenly become catchable again.

Size of Steelhead

Pacific Northwest steelhead vary in size: small ones weigh just three or four pounds, large ones are fifteen to twenty-five pounds, and huge ones are thirty pounds or greater. In the pre-catch-and-release days we killed the fish, and if we wanted to know how big it was we would weigh it before cleaning. Most steelhead rivers are catch-and-release on wild fish and many anglers measure the length, and sometimes the length and girth, of fish they release and try to approximate weights. Although it isn't scientifically sound, because girth dimensions play a large role in calculating accurate weights of fish released, I generally use the "length minus 20 rule" to come up with an approximate weight. The rule is a simple correlation between length and weight. To get an estimated weight for a 29-inch steelhead, subtract 20 inches and you come up with 9 lb. Simple, and this works for the average-girthed steelhead, plus or minus 10 percent, in the 25- to 35-inch range. By using this method we can quickly get an estimate of weight and get the fish back into the river for a speedy release.

However, if your fish looks deep and/or is greater than thirty-five inches long and you want to determine a more accurate weight use Sturdy's formula. Weight in pounds = 0.00133 x (girth) 2 x length (girth and length in inches.) Following is a Sturdy weight chart for large fish.

Sturdy's formula for calculating weight of large fish:

LENGTH

GIRTH	34	35	36	37	38	39	40	41	42	43	44	45	46
16	11.6	11.9	12.3	12.6	12.9	13.3	13.6	14.0	14.3	14.6	15.0	15.3	15.7
17	13.1	13.5	13.8	14.2	14.6	15.0	15.4	15.8	16.1	16.5	16.9	17.3	17.7
18	14.7	15.1	15.5	15.9	16.4	16.8	17.2	17.7	18.1	18.5	19.0	19.4	19.8
19	16.3	16.8	17.3	17.8	18.2	18.7	19.2	19.7	20.2	20.6	21.1	21.6	22.1
20	18.1	18.6	19.2	19.7	20.2	20.7	21.3	31.8	22.3	22.9	23.4	23.9	24.5
21	19.9	20.5	21.1	21.7	22.3	22.9	23.5	24.0	24.6	25.2	25.8	26.4	27.0
22	21.9	22.5	23.2	23.8	24.5	25.1	25.7	26.4	27.0	27.7	28.3	29.0	29.6
23	23.9	24.6	25.3	26.0	26.7	27.4	28.1	28.8	29.5	30.3	31.0	31.7	32.4
24	26.0	26.8	27.6	28.3	29.1	29.9	30.6	31.4	32.2	32.9	33.7	34.5	35.2
25	28.3	29.1	29.9	30.8	31.6	32.4	33.3	34.1	34.9	35.7	36.6	37.4	38.2

For example, my friend, Van Egan, caught his largest-ever steelhead while fishing the Dean River in 1994 after nearly fifty years fly fishing for steelhead. The fish was very long at forty-three inches, but with a twenty-one-inch girth not a bulky, heavy fish for its length. From the summary table, to get the weight follow along the top, marked LENGTH, until you find 43 then go down the side, marked GIRTH, until you find 21 and you get 25.2 lb.

Steelhead populations vary from year to year and are small compared to salmon populations. For example, salmon populations occur in the thousands and tens of thousands with some sockeye and pink populations returning to their home rivers in the millions. Steelhead on the other hand generally number in hundreds with only a few stocks returning in the thousands. To illustrate, before incidental interceptions in the commercial and Native mixed stock fisheries, the Thompson River with three main stocks has a run of 6,000 to

10,000; the Skeena, with about five stocks, has 50,000 to 75,000; and the Chilliwack, with one stock, has a run of about 6,000 to 8,000.

In the mid-1980s we experienced the largest runs in recent years, perhaps larger than the runs of late 1960s and certainly larger than any in the 1970s. Steelhead returns and fishing all along the coast were phenomenal. However, like all cyclic things, the low must come and it is with us now. There is fear the low steelhead populations we now experience, because of decades of indiscriminate catches by market fishers, habitat destruction and the adverse effects of climate change on ocean survival, may not rebound. I hope not, but the warning signs are there. In past years, returns to the Thompson River in some seasons have neared the minimum number of 900 needed to sustain the stocks. East coast Vancouver Island streams have had closures due to poor returns during the 1997 and 1998 seasons.

Steelhead can be caught all year round in the province if you are willing to travel to different locations, and I have taken them in all months but June. Although they are morphologically the same fish, steelhead can be put into two racial groups: winter-run and summer-run. The characteristics that distinguish one race from the other are the timing of river entry and sexual maturity at entry. Summer-run steelhead enter fresh water often hundreds of kilometers from their destination stream through May to early October, and all summer-runs are sexually immature. Winter-run steelhead enter fresh water usually from December to May in a far more advanced state of sexual maturity than their summer-run counterparts, which do most of their maturing in the river during winter and spring. Both races spawn in the spring following their freshwater entry.

Winter-run

Around the beginning of winter, the first winter fish start to show in certain rivers. For example, the Yakoun River on the Queen Charlotte Islands has fish returning from November through May, the Cowichan on Vancouver Island and the

Vedder in the Lower Mainland see returns from December through May. Peak timing of a run is dependent on many things, such as difficulty and length of the journey to the spawning grounds, and often on coastal rivers fish are drawn into the stream by the rains of winter. On some rivers like the Squamish or Wakeman, although they may have fish coming in as early as December, the bulk of the run is drawn in when the snow pack begins to melt, often in April or, if a late freshet, May. Those late-running winter fish are ready to spawn and do so quickly.

Winter steelhead fly fishing is tough. Water temperatures through most of the winter are around the 40°F range and often lower. Fish are not active takers in cold water. The fly fisher must go deep and dirty to be successful. To present the fly properly requires deep wading in cold water and even neoprene waders are often inadequate insulators. However, as winter wanes, usually in March, water temperatures start to move up and fish become more active. Even then the fly fisher needs to probe deeply with his flies. An angler will wonder when the fly stops on its swing whether it is bottom or a steelhead. Once the bottom moves, you won't know if it is a small steelhead or a twenty-pounder. No matter what size, any winter steelhead will leave you shaking with excitement as you play and land the fish. Fly fishers who work hard for winter fish will be rewarded.

Summer-run

Summer-run steelhead are interesting because they have the unique capability to access and use habitat not often available to their winter-returning cousins. These fish make the migration at just the right time. They are able to maximize their own upstream performance since their energy reserves are optimal for strength and endurance. They are not yet hindered by the physiological changes needed for spawning, which can be as long as nine or ten months away. The habitat they are seeking is often above tough canyon chutes and drops and they pick suitable water and river-temperature conditions as river runoff subsides. On small streams this can be as early as May, but on the larger waterways, such as the Fraser and Skeena, migration usually begins in late summer and continues through early fall. Anglers fishing world-renowned summer-run rivers such as the Thompson, Kispiox, Babine, Bulkley and Sustut catch steelhead during the late summer and fall through until the rivers close to angling on December 31. The fish they catch are summer-run steelhead. These fish entered fresh water in the summer and early fall months.

Steelhead are spring spawners and summer-runs return to the river with enough fat reserves to last them until the following spring and to endure the rigors of spawning. A small percentage of steelhead survive spawning, return to the sea and, after regeneration, return to spawn again.

The summer-run steelhead is a fly fisher's fish, especially during the summer and early fall months. Fly fishers will be fishing steelhead when water temperatures in the high 40° to 60°F range, optimum for fish activity. Summer-run steelhead are most active through those temperatures and will rise to take flies on or just below the surface. Whether the catch is a small twenty-incher or a huge fish of twenty pounds-plus, summer-run steelheaders can experience thrills beyond the wildest of dreams when one of those screamers grabs the fly.

River and Stream Tackle and Techniques

In river fishing, the range in fish size can be extreme and many anglers have outfits consisting of matching lines and rods ranging up to #11 to cover that diversity. On many of our steelhead rivers, the average fish may be eight to ten pounds, but most streams will have some fish in the fifteen- to twenty-pound range, with the occasional one even larger. In some rivers, such as the Thompson and Kispiox, fish between fifteen and twenty pounds are common and twenty-plus pounders are frequent. To satisfy my steelhead fly-fishing requirements, I generally use outfits in the #8 to #11 range.

I prefer river fishing to any other and have spent most of the past thirty years in pursuit of summer- and winter-run steelhead. Because of that preference I use special equipment and own three double-handed Spey rods of twelve, fifteen and seventeen and a half feet that throw lines varying from #8 to #11. However, such special tools are costly. If you do lake fishing and have a #7 outfit and are going to do a fair amount of river fishing for fish greater than ten pounds, you could cover most large-fish river fishing with a #9 single-handed outfit with the #7 still water being your back up. Casting a double-handed rod requires both hands, whereas a single-handed rod only requires one hand.

There are a large variety of lines ranging from full floaters, floaters with sink tips to full sinkers suitable for river fishing. A floating line is a must for presenting flies near or on the surface and for upstream sunk-fly fishing. I prefer to Spey cast—a technique developed by Atlantic salmon fisherman on the River Spey in Scotland—even with a single-handed rod, and I use a double-taper floating line instead of the now-popular weight forward. Nonetheless, the weight-forward lines are of good design, cast well and are preferred by many.

Most fish in rivers are bottom dwellers, and although some can be taken on flies on or near the surface, much of the time you must fish down to them. To accomplish this task, a fly fisher should have at least a couple of lines that sink—a fast sinker for slow-moving water and a superfast sinker for deeper and/or fast-moving water. Most fly fishers have abandoned the full sinkers for river fishing and go with sink tips. I make my own sink tips and have extrafast to slow-sink tips ranging from five to sixteen feet in length and loop them onto my double-taper #9, #10 or #11 floater for my steelhead fly fishing. For steelhead you must at times dredge the bottom and many fly fishers use one the Teeney T series of tips for their extrafast tip while others prefer a couple of sink tips from Cortland's or Scientific Anglers' series of lines. Big fish in flowing water usually require a larger capacity reel and a 100 to 200 yards of backing, depending on size of river and fish. Large steelhead on large rivers can use a lot of line.

Perhaps a few words about leaders is appropriate before I close on tackle and move onto steelhead flies. Fishing with a floating line requires a transfer of energy through the fly line and leader to the fly. A tapered leader helps transfer the energy and present the fly properly. However, you don't need costly tapered leaders for sunk-line fishing. For sunk-line, you attach directly to the end of your sink tip or full-sinking line a three- or four-foot section of ten- to fifteen-pound tippet material.

Most steelhead that are catchable will be in three to six feet of water and the purpose of fishing a sunk line is to get the fly down to proper fishing depth quickly. On fast-flowing rivers, if you use a nine- to twelve-foot tapered leader, often your drift is complete by the time the fly has had a chance to sink very deep. By using a short leader attached directly to the fly line, the fly will sink with the line and be down to maximum fishing depth, resulting in a better drift and presentation. Some fly fishers dress their flies with lead and others attach a small split shot to make sure the fly sinks quickly. Flies with lead included in their dressing is permissible on fly-fishing-only waters, but adding external weight to the line is against regulations.

Flies

There are hundreds of steelhead patterns from which a fly fisher can choose, and each locale will have its favorites. One pitfall that distracts many anglers is the change-fly syndrome. This occurs when the fly fishers have so many flies with no criteria for matching conditions with technique they are constantly changing patterns in search of the magic fly. Through many years fishing many rivers, I have surmised that an experienced fly fisher using sound judgment needs only five basic patterns. With a variety of sizes in those basic patterns and if the fisher is able to marry size and pattern to water and light conditions and presentation techniques he or she will spend more productive time fishing.

The five basic patterns include a large fly, such as the General Practitioner, for colored- and/or cold-water conditions, and for use in poor light. It is often, but not exclusively, used on a sunk line. A short-bodied, quick-sinking pattern, such as the Cowichan Coachman, is for use in upstream, sunk fly (nymphtype) presentations. A slim-bodied pattern, such as the Black Spey, is useful for floating-line fishing. A clipped deer hair fly, such as the famous Bomber, is handy for skating across the surface using a floating line and one should have a fly, such as Roderick Haig-Brown's Steelhead Bee, for dry fly fishing. A fly fisher can substitute many patterns for any suggested above as long as the pattern suits the technique. For example, a Woolly Bugger, Egg Sucking Leech or Taylor's Golden Spey will do for the General Practitioner. I prefer the GP because the tail and hackle move enticingly and add life as it sweeps through the current, but if you fancy something less lifelike, the Squamish Poacher is a favorite of many. It certainly sinks quickly. A Woolly Worm can be substituted for the Cowichan Special, a slim-bodied sparsely dressed skunk, Doc Spratley, Purple Peril, or as specified for the Black Spey, a Combo Bug, Lemire's Irresistible, Tom Thumb or Greaseliner for the Bomber, and a Tom Thumb, Grey Wulff or Royal Coachman for the Steelhead Bee.

The Sunk-line Presentation

Most salmonids when observed in their river environment will be seen close to the bottom. And it is this observation, made hundreds of years ago, that has prompted man to fish down to them. Fishing the sunk fly on a down and across sweep with a General Practitioner or substitute is a favorite technique of many fly fishers and one of the most effective ways of catching steelhead with a fly. Before casting the fly, the fisher needs to examine the velocity of the water and configuration of the pool—called reading the water—and then select the best angle for the cast. Usually the cast is about 30° to 60° downstream of the angler and brought across the current and ends up directly below and close to the shore.

Many rivers can be fished effectively with a single-handed rod using the sunk-line technique and it is a favored tool on the smaller rivers. But with the reintroduction of the double-handed fly-rod in the early 1980s, fly fishermen who used it properly, now had a tool that would permit them to cover as much as ninety feet of water with good line control, compared to the fifty or sixty feet of control that single-handed rods permitted.

Accompanying the reintroduction of the two-fisted rods in British Columbia was Spey casting and the double-taper fly line. Not only did this casting technique suit the floating-line presentation, but because of improved line control it made the presentation of the sunk-fly more effective. In 1984, after I became adept at Spey casting, I thought that I could present the fly better, and fish the sunk-fly with more control by looping a section of sinking line onto the end of my double-taper floating line. The results were startling. Spey casts of eighty feet or better were the norm, and on the first day I tried this combination up on the Dean River, six fish took the fly.

The sunk-line is the tool to use when the river is cold and the fish lethargic, or the river is colored and you need to get the fly down to the fish. However, because of changing river velocity, you need to choose a sink-tip that suits the water speed.

Indeed, I remember a couple of days when I used the sunk-line technique with rather surprising results. I had driven to the Thompson River with a couple of friends one day late in November. With just more than two hours of daylight remaining in the day I decided to fish the sunk-line and looped on a seven-foot high-speed, high-density sink tip onto the end of my double-taper #11 floating fly-line. In the next two-and-a-half hours I beached a fine brace of Thompson River steelhead—one 36 ½-inch male and a 35-inch female. Expectations at the start of the day often don't match the results at the end of the day, and I was more than happy with two fish in such short time. You wonder as the day ends what tomorrow holds.

The next day proved better than the afternoon before. Indeed it was, in the first twelve minutes of fishing I had three takes, losing one fish and landing a 34-inch female. Then after lunch, in the next pool, in forty-five minutes fishing with the same combination—Black GP fly and 7-foot sink tip—I landed a brace of 37-inch males. What a day—five takes, one fish lost and three landed.

The down and across presentation used for fishing the sunk-line also suits the floating line technique.

The Floating Line

In the history of fly fishing, this is a relatively new method. It is a very pleasant way to fish for steelhead. It has been called greased-line, floating-line and dry-line fishing. The correct name for it is floating-line fishing. The purpose is to present a fly close to the surface with a line that floats on the surface. This method found its way across the Atlantic to the West Coast in the 1930s when Rod Haig-Brown and General Noel Money used it in the later 1930s for Stamp River summer-run steelhead. Haig-Brown first wrote about it in The Western Angler (1939), and the method has had devotees since that time.

Indeed, I remember when I decided to fly fish the Thompson River. I had heard the water suited the floating-line technique and that is what I used. On a sunny, windy October afternoon I started in on the lower part of the Graveyard Run and worked my way downstream to the rock island. There is a slick at the top end of this water, and I cast my Doc Spratley out and let it come around when I felt what I thought to be a good trout take the fly. It didn't get hooked. My next cast sent my fly through the same water again, I know a fish grabbed it, but all I remember was having my line ripped from the reel and a Thompson steelhead jumping halfway across the river. Gently, I played the fish, and proud I was of the thirty-four-inch female that I landed. Early success brings confidence, and that early Thompson success with the floating line made me a devotee of the technique.

In summer-run streams, like the Dean River, even under optimum water temperatures, because of colored water conditions it is often necessary to use the sunk-line to catch steelhead. However many steelhead streams are almost always clear. With clear-water conditions it is water temperature and depth that dictate fly presentation. A fly fisher must be receptive to use the floating-line technique when clear and warm water conditions prevail. Confidence in method, fly and your own skill is vital for success, and confidence in the floating-line technique will bring rewards. Indeed, fishing the floating line with a slim-bodied fly can be very profitable in water conditions that suit the method.

The Skated or Waked Fly

This is the last of the fly-fishing methods where the fly is cast out either opposite or below the fisher and is brought down and across the current. With both sunk-line and floating-line presentations, the fly is below the surface of the water, but with the skated fly it is not. The main intent of this presentation is to skate a fly over the lie.

This is an old technique dating back to seventeenth-century Britain. The waked or skated fly presentation has had, over the years, many names attached to it. Dibbling, skimming, skittering, waking, riffling, dry-fly fishing and surface-lure are some names that come to mind. All, except dry-fly fishing, are proper terms used to describe the method in which the fly is brought across the surface of water causing a wake. I can't emphasize enough that it is the fly that attracts the attention of the fish, and often a half hitch (the leader looped around the eye so it comes off the side) back of the hook eye ensures the fly will wake even in the calmest of waters.

The waked-fly technique is less consistent than the floating- and sunk-line techniques. You need optimum light conditions with alert fish in water of suitable depth and temperature. However, if you decide to use only this method, you have to fish it at those times of the day when the poorer light conditions exist and, on those bright, sunlit days, using the waked-fly method can severely limit your fishing day.

Although it is perhaps a less productive method, the waked-fly presentation does bring some spectacular rises. Unfortunately, many are false rises, and misses are common when using this technique. To the fish, the dominant target is the apex of the V at the end of the hook, and that is what the fish keys in on. And of course, when it goes after the apex, we end up with a flashy, exciting rise and no hook-up because the fish missed the hook. I remember one evening on the Dean River when I had ten rises to a skated fly with the fly getting the mouth of only three fish: I pricked one, lost one and landed one. You can't catch a fish unless you get it to take the fly into its mouth. Nonetheless, if employed wisely, a Bomber used with the skated-fly technique does bring some of the best thrills there are in steelhead fly fishing. And it does get the attention of traveling fish (some large fish at that). Some fishers I know will fish the waked fly, but when they get a couple of showy rises they will change to a sparsely dressed fly of the right size fished on the floating line and catch the fish.

The waked-fly presentation has become a popular way of fly fishing on many summer-run steelhead streams, and, under the right light and water conditions, it can be effective. One of the reasons it's popular is because all can be seen and because of that it is one of the easiest to learn. However, no matter how exciting the rises, the waked-fly technique will never replace the two more skilled presentation methods of down-and-across fly fishing—the floating and sunk line. All three of these presentations—floating line, sunk line and waked fly—are useful methods, when employed under proper conditions, for covering and searching steelhead water.

Dry Fly

The last two methods—dry fly and upstream sunk fly—suit the single-handed rod, upstream approach to known fish-holding spots and both techniques are more suitable for pools that hold fish for a period.

Although steelhead respond probably much more readily to the waked fly over the dry fly, many steelhead fly fishers do not make a distinction between the waked fly and the dry fly. I do. I have too deep a respect for the British fly fishing roots and masters that preceded me to disregard the work of anglers such as George LaBranche, E. R. Hewitt and especially Roderick Haig-Brown who promoted the dry-fly technique more than any other steelhead fly fisher.

Dry flies were introduced to B.C. about seventy-five years ago on the Capilano River and had followers on that river until construction of the Cleveland Dam in 1954 drowned favored runs. Rod Haig-Brown revitalized the fly in the 1950s and 1960s on the Campbell and Heber rivers and he wrote about that technique in *Fisherman's Summer* (1959) and *Fisherman's Fall* (1964).

John Fennelly's *Steelhead Paradise* is an account of his adventures fly fishing for steelhead in the Skeena watershed and he describes the dry-fly technique well: "When I fish for steelhead with a dry fly, I use exactly the same technique that I would in casting for any other type of trout. I try to get into position about twenty feet below the fish and well off to one side. I then use a 'slack line' or 'curve' cast so as to permit as long a free drift of the fly as possible" (p. 73).

Haig-Brown, who wrote about taking steelhead on dries as early as 1951, and Fennelly, years later, describe similar dry-fly techniques and both realized that fish often came to the fly once it ended its drift and started to wake. In fact a dragged fly often moved fish that were unmovable to the drifted fly. Steelhead fly fishers were quick to adapt and ended up with the down-and-across fly presentation described earlier as the waked-fly technique. The traditional dry-fly technique developed by LaBranche and Hewitt for Atlantic salmon and Haig-Brown for steelhead requires the fly to float drag free.

Upstream Sunk Fly

This is another technique that favors an upstream presentation to fish in known holding waters and is more suitable to the single-handed rod. This technique often works well when fish have been in a pool for a while and won't respond because they are stale or spooky, or the water has cooled and they won't rise. Often steelhead are found in deep holding pools and this is the only technique, using a weighted fly such as a Cowichan Special, to get down to the bottom-hugging fish. Usually a weighted fly is cast above the holding spot and allowed to sink down to the level of the fish so it does not have to move much to take the fly.

To Sum Up

Indeed, opportunities exist on Northwest steelhead streams to use all five techniques and variations of those techniques described in this discourse. However, combining the correct fly pattern with presentation and water and light conditions are critical for consistent success on any steelhead river. The following table provides some guidelines on marrying water temperature and clarity, light conditions, technique and pattern. However, nothing in fly fishing is absolute —this is only a guide, but it will get you started on the right track.

Conditions and Techniques

WATER (°F)	RIVER TYPE	TECHNIQUE	FLY TYPE
Less than 48°	1. Run 2. Pocket	1. Sunk-line 2. Upstream-sunk	1. GP-type 2. Nymph-type
Comments The colder the water the slower and closer to the fish the fly needs to be presented. The floating-line technique can be effective in the high 40°s.			
48° to 55°	1. Run 2. Run 3. Run 4. Pocket	1. Sunk-line 2. Floating-line 3. Skated-fly 4. Upstream-sunk	1. GP-type 2. to 8s sparse 3. Bomber-type 4. Nymph-type
Comments 1. If water visibility is poor use the sunk-line all day. 2. Use larger fly in lower temperatures. Using a floating line with sparsely dressed fly can be the only effective way of catching steelhead during the midday light. 3. Nymph-type presentation can be very effective for seen fish that have settled in, i.e., stale fish.			
55° to 65°	1. Run 2. Run 3. Run 4. Pocket 5. Pocket	1. Sunk-line 2. Floating-line 3. Skated-fly 4. Upstream-sunk 5. Dry-fly	1. GP-type 2. sparse 2 to 8s 3. Bomber-type 4. Nymph-type 5. Steelhead Bee-type
Comments 1. If water visibility is poor, use the sunk-line all day. 2. Use larger floating-line type fly in lower temperatures. Floating-line can be the only effective way of catching steelhead during the midday light on sun-baked runs. Large GP-type fly can be effective fished with a floating line in poor light conditions such as those found during the early morning, late evening or on overcast days. 3. Skated presentation is effective during poor light conditions or on shaded portions of run. It is not effective during the heat of the day on sun-baked runs. 4. Nymph-type presentation can be very effective with stale fish in known holding spots. 5. The natural drift dry fly is best tried at the higher temperature regimes.			

More Great Hancock House Fishing Titles

Steelhead
Barry M. Thornton
ISBN 0-88839-370-9
5½ x 8½, 192 pp.

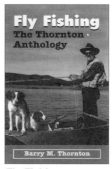

Fly Fishing:
Thornton Anthology
Barry M. Thornton
ISBN 0-88839-426-8
5½ x 8½, 192 pp.

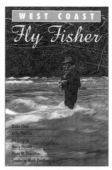

West Coast Fly Fisher
Mark Pendlington
ISBN 0-88839-440-3
5½ x 8½, 152 pp.

Saltwater Flyfishing
for Pacific Salmon
Barry M. Thornton
ISBN 0-88839-268-0
5½ x 8½, 168 pp.

Mooching: The Salmon
Fisherman's Bible
David Nuttall
ISBN 0-88839-097-1
5½ x 8½, 184 pp.

Trout Fishing
Ed Rychkun
ISBN 0-88839-338-5
5½ x 8½, 120 pp.

West Coast
River Angling
Eric Carlisle
ISBN 0-88839-212-5
5½ x 8½, 192 pp.

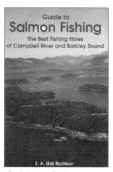

Guide to Salmon
Fishing
Ed Rychkun
ISBN 0-88839-305-9
5½ x 8½, 96 pp.

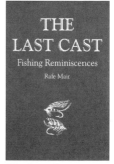

The Last Cast:
Fishing Reminiscences
Rafe Mair
ISBN 0-88839-346-6
5½ x 8½, 160 pp.